Sacred Power,
Holy Surrender

Living A Spiritual Power Dynamic

Edited by Raven Kaldera

Sacred Power,
Holy Surrender

Living a Spiritual Power
Dynamic

Edited by Raven Kaldera

Alfred Press
Hubbardston, Massachusetts

Alfred Press
12 Simond Hill Road
Hubbardston, MA 01452

Sacred Power, Holy Surrender: Living A Spiritual Power Dynamic
© 2011 by Raven Kaldera
ISBN 978-0-9828794-2-9
Cover photo by Lee Harrington © 1996

"Of Mastery And Service" and "Of Slavery And Service" by Lee
Harrington were originally published in *Sacred Kink: The Eightfold
Paths of BDSM,* edited by Lee Harrington.
"Finding The Slow Path" by Joshua Tenpenny previously
appeared in *Spirit of Desire,* edited by Lee Harrington.

Printed in cooperation with
Lulu Enterprises, Inc.
860 Aviation Parkway, Suite 300
Morrisville, NC 27560

To my slaveboy Joshua,
without whom I could not have walked this road.

To all those who chose to share their stories,
ripping open the raw soul to pour across the page,
I thank you for your generosity
and so does the next generation.

Contents

Walking Together

Foreword: This Path We Walk

I come from a spiritual perspective that sees everything as having an inherently sacred nature. For me, the sacred is not just found in some other divine dimension, but it is everywhere—in our bodies, in our hearts, in the natural world around us. When it comes to human activities, we may not be expressing our lives in the most sacred or spiritually whole way possible, but the underlying urges of humanity are sacred. That includes sex, and it also includes relationships.

I've believed that sexuality was sacred from an early age, when I first experienced it as a way to touch the Divine. It took me a while, however, to fight through the social messages and be able to accept that my form of sexuality was also sacred, or at least could be expressed that way. In much of my religious faith, it is assumed that "sacred sexuality"—and by extension, sacred relationship—was tender, nurturing, and above all egalitarian. BDSM-style sex was seen as, at best, a distraction from the "real" path of spiritual sex and relationship, a kind of immature cul-de-sac that would ideally be outgrown, and at worst a perpetuation of harmful and abusive ideology.

I refused to believe that. I jumped into researching the sacred aspects of "kinky" sex and physical ordeal, both historically and through the growing number of personal accounts of people's experiences, and the culmination of that was my book *Dark Moon Rising*. However, when I would talk to people about what I'd discovered, I found that it was far easier to get them to see spiritual value in being flogged or even going up on hooks (after all, it was similar to what those people in *National Geographic* were doing) than in deliberately inegalitarian relationships. The practices of D/s and M/s were far too suspiciously reflective of all the nonconsensual and negative power dynamics forced on people throughout history, and even today. Even within the demographic of people who were happily flogging one another, power dynamics were mistrusted as being too likely to result in abuse. People who would play with roles for a two-hour scene were mistrustful of those who tried to have limited full-time D/s, and those people were mistrustful of full-time master/slave relationships, and even some of the people in the latter demographic were mistrustful of intensely controlling owner/property relationships. And what people can't trust even to be remotely safe or healthy, they generally aren't likely to accept as a vehicle for transformative spirituality.

And yet ... just as, years before, I'd had people walk up to me and shyly or inarticulately or passionately tell me about how their SM scene took them somewhere that was spiritual in nature, now, a decade later, people are beginning to walk up to me and speak about how they are finding spiritual fulfillment in their deliberately inegalitarian relationships. My slaveboy and I began, tentatively, to give workshops about our ideas of spiritual D/s and M/s, and the rooms were usually packed. We feared that our experience would be too personal, too specific, too exotic to click with other people who had only this style of relationship in common with us, but when we spoke about it we saw people in the audience nodding their heads.

I believe that the spark that instigated this slowly growing flame is mindfulness. When we as a demographic—and by this I mean the entire BDSM demographic—began to deconstruct what we do and train people to do it safely, we laid the groundwork for a paradigm of open education, practice, and mindfulness, instead of shamefully flailing away in the dark and hoping that no one got hurt. The well- trained top and the bottom who knew how to communicate their limits—and that they were allowed to do so—set the foundation for the dominant who holds to a code of ethics and honor, and the submissive who knows that they have the right to choose their dominant carefully, and leave if they are unhappy. We began, as a demographic, to talk about how to have healthy power exchanges. We began to think about it carefully, and sometimes to argue. We taught each other how to negotiate and what we had the right to expect. We compared different levels of power and control, and discovered our differences in what levels of control any of us wanted or needed. We began, in other words, to apply mindfulness to our inegalitarian relationships.

This was in sharp contrast to all the inegalitarian sexual relationships in history. While some couples with power dynamics like to compare themselves to or even romanticize historical slavery or "traditional" marriage, what we do with modern consensual and heavily negotiated power dynamics is nothing like this. In my book *Power Circuits: Polyamory In A Power Dynamic*, I wrote about those who claim that this is "just like being a 1950s housewife":

> When looking at the M/s practices of the people I respect, regardless of gender combinations, I find that we put a great deal of thought into the headspace and well-being of our slaves. We dig into their minds and ponder their thoughts. We communicate constantly. We go to a huge amount of trouble to figure out what's best for them, and how to get them to come to a place of comfort with our wishes and expectations. We make sure that they are suitable for this life before we take charge of them. We worry about our honor, and acting rightly toward our slaves, and earning—and keeping— their trust.
>
> "Traditional marriage", of the type where husband had full chattel rights over wife, was not anything like that. The religious and civil rulings that hemmed in the wife made it irrelevant. The husband did not need to earn her trust—she was often handed to him willy-nilly as a girl and could not leave because the community would bring her back. He did not take her feelings into account, nor was he encouraged to by society and male "gender norms" of the time—in fact, he was discouraged from this. Her submission to whatever situation she found herself nonconsensually (and possibly unhappily) in was maintained not merely (or even mostly) by him, but by her upbringing and the

other female members of her family. Even if she was miserable and unsuited for that life, he was not required to do anything about it. (Romantic love was not necessarily always an expected thing, either.)

Even in a kindly and well-suited marriage, the sort of transparency and communication and shaping that experienced M/s practitioners do was unheard of. Intimacy was not a high value in relationships—following the social rules was instead. Couples might go their entire lives not speaking to each other about their inner lives, and that was normal, and it worked because the expectations were low and the social rules held everything in place—like a supporting web, or like a prison, depending on the person.

It is the last 40 years, from the sexual revolution on, that influences our approach to M/s relationships today more than many would like to admit. The emphasis on equality and the shaking off of social norms placed a greater emphasis on communication and emotional intimacy (as being normal) to replace those bonds, and we utilize that today, those "forced" relationship skills. The kind of master/slave relationship techniques that are discussed in detail at support groups and conferences by M/s teachers and mentors, these would have been unnecessary and unthinkable in former times. Some people may idealize and euphemize the past in ways that are unrealistic, but the truth is that we have more to thank from the sexual revolution than from its preceding eras for most of what makes modern M/s work.

So what does this have to do with spirituality? Simple. In my experience, the more mindfulness that one puts into one's important human processes, the more likely it is that a spiritual awakening of some kind will come upon you. The one does seem to lead to the other rather naturally, as most religions will tell you. The more we scrutinize, perfect, and purify our attitudes and motivations around any subject, the more likely it is that it will become a door through which that sacred energy will flow.

One thing that jumped out at me as I edited this anthology was that so many of the titles of these essays had the word "path" in them. It was a theme repeated again and again. The metaphor of a road, a spiritual journey walked together by two people, seems to be an archetypal part of this ... well, yes, again I'm wanting to use a word like "quest" or something similar, which is really the same thing, isn't it? Certainly many spiritual traditions and personal experiences use that metaphor, but it seems to me that this context is the most frequently I've seen it used to describe the spiritualizing of an intimate relationship. Why is this a "path"? My first instinct is to say that we've been at it for a decade and the further we go, the more we realize we have yet to learn. It's a work in progress, not a trick that you manage to pull off and then you're "there".

The essays in this book are written by a variety of people, straight and gay, male and female and in between. Some are currently in spiritual power dynamics and some were at one time, but no longer. Some live fairly conservative lives, aside from their power dynamic; others are sex radicals. Some move within the framework of a specific religion and some prefer to create their own unique spiritual spaces. Some are at the beginning of their path and some have been on it for many years. Some have limited power dynamics and some have very intense ones that permeate every aspect of life. Some live with their partners and some don't. Some consider the master/mistress to be the slave's spiritual superior and some do not. In spite of all these differences, we all manage to find a direction that sounds oddly, beautifully familiar to each other. It seems that the further we walk, the less our differences matter to the journey.

This path is not for everyone. I would never claim that there was something wrong with a power dynamic relationship that was mutually satisfying to all parties involved but had no spiritual component to it. Not everyone is meant to do this, and that's all right; just as most people in the world are not suited to any sort of power dynamic relationship and would do better to be egalitarian. It's not necessary for everyone's happiness, but it is necessary for the well-being of some people. This book is for those who are yearning for it, those who are doing it, and those who are merely curious as to what we're talking about. It's not a handbook so much as a series of snapshots of the road signs that some of us have passed on our journeys together. It won't give you a map, but it might help you recognize the landmarks as you pass them, and help you to trust that you're on the way.

In the name of sacred power and holy surrender, be thou blessed. We certainly have been. And it's only right to pass it on.

RAVEN KALDERA
MAY 2011

Putting Together
the Pieces

Note: When we wrote our book Dear Raven And Joshua: Questions And Answers About Master/Slave Relationships, *my slaveboy Joshua and I developed a writing style where we went back and forth in a dialogue and answered questions from both the dominant and submissive sides. We got a lot of good feedback about this approach from people who appreciated seeing our interlocking perspectives, and so we repeated it in the essay in the last section of this book, "The Path Of Devotion". In this first section we're going to do it yet again, because there is so much that we have to cover, but it's important that both of us has their authentic voice heard. So we thank you for your patience in reading this section, and we hope that it is concise in its information.*

Some of the material that we discuss here has been previously discussed in a few of our other books, but this is the first time it's all been put together in one place.

Chain of Command

Raven:

It doesn't look all that special. After one gets over the shock of seeing a relationship where one person makes all the major decisions and the other person is pledged to obey them in all things, one might notice that it doesn't look hugely different, on the outside, than most other life companionships. Perhaps there is less banter and a little more seriousness, but that could be true for anyone. Perhaps there are far fewer arguments, but it's not true that there are none. I don't float around in long robes making wise pronouncements and calling him "Grasshopper" while he trails after me, basking in my holy presence. Mostly we're busy with other things, and we have to make space and time for mindfulness. The spirit will enter, but only if you pay attention and keep the door open, and we're not always perfect about doing that.

How did this begin? In 2002, I entered into a master/slave relationship with Joshua. I was a Neo-Pagan priest and a Northern Tradition shaman of many years by that point, and I tried hard to live my life by what my spiritual path had taught me. I needed, very much, to have no separation between the "spiritual" parts of my life and the "mundane" parts. That included this relationship, which was turning out to be so different from any other relationship I'd ever lived. I wanted it, desperately, wanted it with a hunger that ran deep and hot and hard ... and it was terrifying. It meant taking on full responsibility for another human being.

I'd been a parent before, so to some extent I'd already done that ... but with a child, the entire goal is to get them to adulthood with as much preparedness as possible, and then send them out into the world. Everything is aimed, subtly or otherwise, at that moment of leaving. For a master/slave relationship, the opposite is true: we would be working toward becoming more and more integrated, until he was fitted in as an extension of my life, my body, my heart, my mind, my soul, my karmic record.

I knew, also, that I would be judged. I serve a Goddess (of the ancient Norse variety), and I am very much Her slave, in that I am bound to serve Her with all parts of my being for the rest of my life. I'd asked Her, two years before Joshua came into my life, for someone like him. I laid the little leather bracelet that said "Raven's Boy"—which had already adorned the wrists of more than one failed experiment—on an altar and asked, formally. "I am obviously no good at picking the right one. Please help me. If you send him over, I will take good care of him." Two years later, Joshua came into my life through a series of bizarre coincidences that could only be a cosmic set-up, and I knew that my petition had been granted. Now I had to keep up my end of the bargain. This is a chain of command, and I knew that I would be watched. As I treated him, so I would be treated. If I abused the privilege of having a slave, She would make me sorry.

To make this less personal to me, I'll say that I've spoken to other M/s couples who are creating their relationship as a spiritual path, and it does seem to be the case that when you announce to the Universe that this is now more than merely recreational, the Universe sits up and holds you to your word. I've said before that there is nothing "less" about having a "merely" recreational, loving, and fulfilling M/s relationship, and I'll say that again. In fact, it's harder to run a M/s relationship as a spiritual discipline, and this is one of the reasons why.

We've seen it again and again: in a non-spiritual M/s relationship, if the master/mistress abuses their authority, any consequences will come directly from the damage that it does to their partner, and to the peace and longevity of their time together. It may take quite a while for this damage to accumulate. In contrast, once a couple has set their intention to walk this spiritual discipline together, the Universe goes out of its way to arrange consequences in a hurry. The dominant who abuses their power sends a direct message: "This is how I think people should behave when they have power over some hapless person," and the Universe will quickly arrange a situation for them to find out what that feels like. Perhaps within days, they will be stopped by a police officer who holds that opinion as well. You may laugh, but it's real. It happens, so be careful what you ask for—and what you do once you've got it.

Joshua:

When I first got involved with Raven I wasn't particularly spiritual, but I knew that he was, and I liked that he was deeply committed to living rightly according to his beliefs. He didn't express any interest in educating me about his religion, which struck me as unusual until I learned that his religious community has a strict prohibition against trying to convert anyone. Even after I had a number of profoundly transformative spiritual experiences and became involved in his church of my own volition, he maintained a very hands-off approach for many years. It was frustrating, because at the time I just wanted him to tell me what I ought to do and believe, but it forced me to look deeply at a lot of spiritual issues and come to my own understanding of them.

For one thing, I believe in karma, which is to say that I believe in a natural force dictating that what you do comes back to you, in a way which is designed to teach you something. Each of us has our own karmic load to carry, lessons to learn, responsibility to take for our actions. The Universe expects—or hopes, at least—that we will make good decisions on our own.

But something happens when someone turns themselves willingly over to someone else. The master adds the slave's karma to their own, ending up with two persons' worth of karma, two persons' worth of cosmic responsibility, and two persons' worth of payment for failure. And yet, in the weird math of karma, the slave still has all their own karma. They don't get to give it all away and have no responsibility. The slave still has to be a responsible, disciplined, self-aware human being, at the same time that they are turning themselves over to their master. This means that there's just more karma to go around, and it's more important that both parties try harder to be their highest selves. This is a path with a steep learning curve, and it's not for everyone ... but the rewards are amazing.

Being and Doing

Raven:

What are the criteria for a spiritually-focused power dynamic? In this book, you will see a lot of different assumptions about that. Our personal dynamic works on the assumption that both of us are strongly dedicated to our respective spiritual paths, but some of the authors in this book will discuss how this can work when one party (usually the master) doesn't have a strong spiritual focus at all. However, this is a much more difficult situation than one where both people do have a spiritual focus as part of their life—not impossible, but a rougher road.

Should it be done only with people whose spiritual practices come from the same context? Not necessarily, although again that does make it easier. If the partners have very different practices, it will require a lot of negotiation on both parts, and the master must take care not to interfere with the slave's practices or attempt to pressure them into converting. Each should not only respect but appreciate the other's path, and be willing to understand it in depth even if they don't choose to practice it, or they will not be able to aid and assist one another properly. It's also much easier when both people have a similar understanding about following one's spiritual path, and can commiserate and help each other through. That's useful for couples regardless of power dynamics, but it's especially useful when the dominant must make informed decisions about the sub's life that may impact their practices. Regardless of their personal practices, however, it is more important that both have similar ideas about the spiritual responsibilities of their respective positions, and how those work together.

Sometimes a would-be slave asks us whether they should keep their own spiritual path separate, or whether they should attempt to integrate it entirely into the (future or present) M/s relationship. I ask them this: Do you trust this dominant to have better judgment about your own spiritual path than you do? If the answer is "No" (or "I've never met anyone I would trust with that, and I don't think I ever will"), then it's perfectly acceptable to keep the major decisions about your spiritual life between yourself and the Powers That Be. Just make sure that it's all laid down that way in the early negotiations.

If your answer is "Yes", there's no problem—just do it. If your answer is "That's what I'm looking for," then my best suggestion for you is to pray. If you don't believe in personified deities, then just ask the Universe to send the right person to you. It may take a while—it took almost two years for the Powers That Be to get Joshua to my doorstep—but it works. However, if years are going by and it's not happening, that may be the Universe's way of telling you that this is not what you're supposed to be doing. The disciple's path is not for everyone. There's also the possibility that if you're on the right spiritual path, it can be so all-encompassing that it tends to edge out everything else, including relationships. The only good answer is to find a way to build the relationship into the path, so to speak; to dance its dance in such a way that it supports and enhances the path rather than draws attention away from it.

On the other side of things, occasionally a master/slave relationship can become an excuse for avoiding some challenging aspect of one person's spiritual path. When you have a genuine calling, anything that distracts you from that calling tends to fall away no matter how painful that is for everyone involved. As a person goes deeper into their spiritual path, ambivalent situations tend to reach a crisis point, because the person needs to get through their baggage in order to go further. Throwing yourself into such an emotionally arresting dynamic (and it's as possible to fall in love with the dynamic as with the other person) can provide a good distraction for the desperate. The problem is that, as Caroline Myss says, "God doesn't need your permission to make you live your life." When power dynamics are used in this way, the Universe often does something to break up the harmony that the spiritual runaway is taking such comfort in.

Joshua:

I'll say up front that it is really tough to balance a spiritual calling with full-time M/s when the dominant isn't part of that calling. It's possible, and it has been good to hear from people who are doing just that, but it's a hard way to go. Both spirituality and M/s are processes that tend expand to fill and overflow whatever container you provide for them. Either one has the potential to transform every area of your life, making it hard to keep things neatly separated.

For me personally, it would be very challenging to submit fully to someone who isn't my spiritual superior in some meaningful way. I have a strong need for the "disciple's path" as part of my relational archetypes, and it is both fulfilling and comforting to have someone to guide me in this way. If I hadn't found this with my master, I likely would have found a more conventional sort of spiritual superior outside of a master/slave context, and put much less spiritual focus on this relationship.

That said, not all s-types want their M-type to be their spiritual superior. Some prefer to develop their spiritual relationship independently, without the intervention of another human being, even one they are serving, and that's fine. Some have a pre-existing relationship with a spiritual teacher or clergyperson. Each of us has a different path. Some may only need someone who is as spiritually dedicated and committed as they are, and can equally shoulder the burden of integrating their relationship into the path, and might be just fine with a master who isn't their spiritual superior. They may see their process of spiritual transformation as a collaboration between spiritual equals, with complementary rather than hierarchical roles.

However, many s-types seem reluctant to accept anyone short of a saint as their spiritual superior. While that may come from an inflated sense of their own spiritual development, I think it comes more often from the fear of putting your life in the hands of a fallible human being. Of course this is scary, but the first time the master makes a big mistake is a milestone for the relationship, not its inevitable end. If a solid foundation of trust has been established, it can be an opportunity for the s-type to come to a more mature and realistic respect for their master, rather than a childlike insistence that their master be perfect.

I'm a bit uneasy about spiritually-focused master/slave relationships where the s-type considers themselves to be substantially more spiritually developed than the master. I've seen that work, with a slave who humbly guided the master in their spiritual development, but more frequently I've seen it become a source of unresolvable conflict. The most common pattern is where the M-type feels obligated to defer entirely to the slave's judgment on anything even vaguely connected to their spirituality. Then when some (perhaps trivial) aspect of the s-type's spirituality inevitably comes into conflict with the M-type's will, it puts the s-type in the position of choosing between their spirituality and obedience. Complicating things further, there is generally a fair amount of room for personal interpretation in spiritual matters, and the tendency to slant one's interpretation in self-serving ways is a challenge faced by spiritual seekers of all types. Even on a subconscious level, s-types may use their spirituality to avoid the more challenging aspects of their master/slave relationship.

The other source of my uneasiness with "spiritually superior" s-types is that their perception of themselves as spiritually superior can be an ego-driven perception that may not reflect the reality of their situation. I've met quite a few couples where the dominant did not identify as a "spiritual" or "religious" person, but showed a deep sense of honor, purpose, and dedication to certain ideals, while the "spiritual" submissive was very invested in the cultural trappings of some spiritual tradition, without living that tradition quite so deeply.

Even if the s-type's assessment is accurate, that feeling of superiority over their master in such a deeply meaningful area of life can undermine their respect for their master, and make it exceedingly difficult to approach the ego-surrender which is one of the great mysteries of spiritual submission.

Another motivation for an s-type to submit to their master in spiritual matters is something I learned from the *Rule of St. Benedict*. It warns young monks not to go off to live on their own, away from the direct supervision of an experienced superior. Without years of experience in setting the ego aside by following the direction of another, their interpretation of God's will is self-serving, The monks may be quite sincere, but they underestimate the cleverness of the ego. "What pleases them, they call holy. What they despise, they call sinful." It doesn't take an exceptionally high level of spiritual attainment to notice someone else doing this, but it is incredibly difficult to see it in yourself. We are all uniquely blind to our own biases. In this way, any reasonably insightful and honest master can be a valuable spiritual guide to the s-type, provided the s-type is willing to listen.

Service

Raven:

Service is not respected in modern Western society. We have ambivalent and conflicted feelings about one person serving another in a formal, negotiated, subservient role. Most modern people claim to hate the idea of being told what to do or of having our right to do anything we want restricted, and outright resent having to defer to someone based on their position. Some people complain about authority, or even rebel against it reflexively simply because it's there. What this means, socially, is that service is generally devalued, as are service workers. They tend to be low-paid and treated rudely, and it is assumed that their jobs require little in the way of skill, perceptiveness, or intelligence. When it comes to personal service jobs such as the waiter or the housewife, we tend to assume that no one could actually enjoy such a job, and everyone currently doing them are merely biding their time until they can get "better" jobs. Those would be the ones where you are on the ordering side of the lunch counter, rather than being on the side where they cook the fries. Actually doing the order-taking is seen as degrading by definition. We encourage this attitude in every new generation, and then we wonder why they are surly to us from behind the counter, forget our ketchup, steal from our houses as they clean the floors, laugh at the idea of community service, and eventually grow up to hire desperate illegal immigrants to do the work that they found so belittling.

Modern attitudes toward service have a long history of downward mobility. Ancient and medieval Europe had plenty of customs around human interaction that we would consider unhealthy and repellent (such as nonconsensual slavery), but they did have a healthier and more practical ideal of service than we do. Service was not limited merely to a class of rich folk who never served others and a class of poor folk who were never served themselves. Since everyone lived as part of a hierarchy, everyone (except the very top and the very bottom) was expected to experience both serving and being served. If a duke came to visit the earl, the earl or his son might serve the duke supper with his own hands, to show him honor. The duke himself might have served the king a week ago, and so on up and down the chain. Beyond this, there were clerics and monastics who—ideally, anyway—served God, often by serving the people, for spiritual reasons.

Many M/s couples have been inspired by Victorian-era service and hierarchy, modeling their households on some version thereof. While service had evolved and stratified by the Victorian era into something more class-limited than in the medieval era, there was still a strong value of taking pride in one's service and one's "place"; one strove to do a good job at whatever service task one was assigned, even if it was invisible, and while one also strove to climb the ladder and do better (the butler and the housekeeper were usually the top of the service ladder), it wasn't seen as degrading to spend one's life honorably in service. The Victorian era also saw the preference for household service personnel to remain unmarried and childless (and theoretically celibate), an odd echo of a monastic life in many ways.

In the strong push to gain personal independence and social worth for all types of people, service has been the baby thrown out with all the dirty bathwater. We can't go back to a medieval or Victorian society, and we would not want to for other reasons— behaviors that it is good that we've disposed of—but we can certainly learn to take another look at service. One of the points on a checklist for the ideal dominant that Joshua and I have given single-and-seeking submissives is to find out how they receive service and treat service personnel. Are they comfortable receiving service, or do they fidget with discomfort and try to do it themselves, taking the bag away from the cashier and bagging their own groceries? Are they polite to service personnel, or do they insult waiters, snap at cashiers, and yell at gas station attendants? These can be red flags, because someone who can't treat service people courteously and let them do their jobs may secretly (or not-so-secretly) think that service is degrading. This often spills over into contempt for the people doing the serving, and the seeking submissive is going to bear the brunt of that attitude.

We modern folks could use a bit of reeducation in the value of service, either one-on-one service interactions—paid or otherwise— or serving society and those less well off. To put oneself—even temporarily—in a selfless position for the sake of making others happier and more comfortable has always been a worthy goal. For it to be a spiritual goal, however, the rewards have to come not in the form of obligations and favors owed or returned by those for whom you sacrifice, but in the form of intangibles—pleasure at making others happy, pride in doing a good job, and/or positive feelings from being part of the larger goal of making even a small part of the world easier rather than harder.

Ironically, those who choose a path of dedicated service and submission can face mistrust and denigration from outside society. Outsiders to power-dynamic lifestyles ask why some people are drawn to this much more intense and personal form of service. Why choose to serve a single, flawed human being rather than serving humanity impersonally, or—for the more religiously inclined— serving Deity directly, with no human middleman? That's the question that makes many critics of spiritual power dynamics turn up their noses. Surely the world would be a better place, they point out, if you dedicated yourself to feeding the hungry instead of slavishly cooking dinner for one individual?

Our answers have often been difficult in coming, but these are some of them: Reverence for and obedience to deity in whatever form you see it is generally part of the religious experience, but some people need a more concrete representation. Perhaps the voice of deity is indistinguishable from their own internal monologue. Perhaps they need someone more physically present and watchful in their lives to guide them, and give them head-pats and ass-kicking when necessary. Perhaps they need structure and discipline, and they need it in a personal one-on-one way rather than from an impersonal group. Perhaps their religion doesn't have a monastic order, they are not fit for the military, and they don't wish to join a cult. Perhaps they are highly sexual and want that incorporated into their gift of service, which is more safely done with a partner than doing the sacred prostitute archetype indiscriminately in this society.

Living a life of simplicity and spiritual discipline can involve a certain amount of depersonalizing the self, which some people do better than others. Those who are prone to doing it badly—or shallowly, only on a surface level—may do better with the constant scrutiny of a one-on-one power-dynamic relationship, where they are not allowed to get away with superficial submission. Those for whom it is important to retain some measure of their uniqueness might find impersonal service a hard road; with a more personal service relationship you may be an object, but at least you are (or ought to be) an *individual and valued* object. Or it may be that annihilation of the individual self is just not their job this time around, and they need stimulation, people, and personal love. Whatever the reasons, some people simply find personal service to one human being more valuable to their own spiritual growth than any amount of abstract impersonal love.

Joshua:

The rejection of service positions often seems to be as much about the requirement for deferential behavior as it is about the service itself. Aside from high-end businesses, the current service ideal in the States is cheerful, helpful, and friendly, rather than respectful and deferential. It's the compromise of our supposed egalitarian society between giving good service and making service personnel feel like a social inferior. However, to be an s-type is to serve from a place of willingness to be a social inferior, at least with certain people or in specific interactions.

Walking this narrow path requires releasing the outer-world ideals that you may have been carrying and shifting your assessment of what is most important. For example, s-types often end up doing work that is devalued by society. They might fill a role as a personal secretary or assistant, or—even more socially dismissed—a traditional housewife, regardless of gender. Rather than feeling like the work is "beneath" them, the s-type can learn about finding honor in simple labor, satisfaction in any honorable work that needs doing, and doing one's best at any assigned task. Even repetitive and "mind-numbing" labor can be meditative—there is no essential difference between raking sand in a Zen garden and vacuuming the living room, as long as the person doing it understands that.

Sexual service is often included in this arrangement, which may be difficult for many people to see as a spiritually meaningful act. In many transcendence-focused spiritual paths, sex is seen as a hindrance to spiritual development, and often the most dangerous of the "worldly" pleasures. In fact, this is probably one of the first issues that comes to mind when people hear us talk about this— "Being a sex object is a spiritual path?" However, the objection comes largely from the unhealthy emphasis our society places on sexuality. Offering one's body as a service, whether in the role of the Sacred Whore or simply as surrender, can be a powerful offering. It doesn't make a difference how fetishistic or conventional the sex is. If you have the right context, there is no such thing as degrading sex in this relationship; it is just service, no more humiliating than cleaning the floor, and probably more fun.

Since we are speaking of humiliation and degradation, we should also speak of humility. It is very important not to confuse the first two with the second one, and even more important not to confuse humility with self-loathing. Ideally, a slave should feel that it is fitting and proper for them to do the work that is given to them, but not because they aren't capable of anything "more important". Doing any service competently and with joy is worthy work, and to do it should give you greater self-esteem.

On the other side of humility is the problem of pride, which usually shows up as the servant becoming rigidly invested in a particular concept of perfect service, regardless of whether this is actually the will of the master. With an inexperienced master, the servant can actually convince them, if only for a while, that this is the "right way" to do something. If the servant fixates on things the master isn't particularly invested in, or they happen to have very similar tastes, this might not cause much of a problem. But eventually the master is likely to come up against something that is at odds with the servant's "right way", and there will be a great upheaval. I can't stress strongly enough that if the s-type believes that things should be done one way and the M-type believes that the process should happen differently, the s-type needs to let it go. One submissive woman said that every time she comes up against this issue, she asks herself, "Is anyone going to die if I do things his way?" So far, the answer has always been no. If the s-type cannot find fulfillment in providing the type of service desired by the M-type, or the s-type believes the M-type is continually unable to make reasonable decisions, both need to reassess whether they are right for each other. However, if the relationship and the power dynamic basically works and is fulfilling, and the s-type is just stuck rigidly on Being Right on some subject, then it is time to practice the discipline of letting go and surrendering the ego.

Monasticism

Joshua:

There's a funny thing that happens when a slave surrenders deeply to their enslavement. Even submissives who aren't very spiritual to start with can suddenly find themselves describing their experience of in terms that sound a lot like a mystic on an ascetic path. Spirituality can sneak up on a slave in that way. After all, it is a path of letting go, giving up the ego, learning to be adaptable to any hardship, and searching for serenity in serving others. Some religions stress this as the ideal path for everyone. I can't comment on that, but it certainly is my path.

M/s couples look to many different models for inspiration for their power dynamics. Sometimes it's a military model, sometimes it's a historical one, sometimes one out of popular fantasy. Sometimes the model is one of spiritual renunciation, often borrowed from monastic orders. For example, in his household manual *The Order For Discipline And Service*, the late Jack McGeorge drew inspiration from the Benedictine Rule, calling his newer slaves "postulants" and "oblates". In monastic communities, the entire lives of the individuals involved may be heavily controlled, up to and including their sexuality, their clothing and hairstyles, the possessions that they are allowed to own, and their daily work. Suffice it to say here that if no one was ever drawn to a path of willingly giving up certain freedoms in pursuit of an intangible goal, no one would ever join these organizations. However, monasticism is being one of a crowd, faceless, whereas personal service in a power dynamic relationship is often intensely personal, one-on-one with people who see each other deeply. It is a different branch of the same path.

I have a very strong monastic streak. Life as a monk gives you very little free will, and that isn't at all scary or unpleasant to me. It is a very narrow path, sacrificing breadth of experience for depth of experience, and it is similar in many ways to a power-dynamic relationship. The simplest personal freedoms are stripped away; you do not get to choose what you eat or wear or when you get up, and little consideration is likely to be given to what you are in the mood to do at any given time. This is not done to cause suffering, but to provide focus and remove distractions. St. Benedict explains the intent in the prologue to the Benedictine Rule: "We are, therefore, about to found a school of the Lord's service, in which we hope to introduce nothing harsh or burdensome. But even if, to correct vices or to preserve charity, sound reason dictates anything that turns out somewhat stringent, do not at once fly in dismay from the way of salvation, the beginning of which cannot but be narrow."

The restrictions don't need to be intentionally harsh; it is just that everything which does not support the goal of rendering service and obedience to your master or mistress can be stripped away. Surrendering the will is a valuable lesson, a way of taming your ego. It is too easy to get caught up in satisfying your own whims, and too easy to form a definition of "self" based on trivial preferences. Having this stripped away is actually very liberating. I would much rather be subject to my master's will than to my own petty emotional drives.

It's surprising how many traditional rules of monasticism resemble "slave" rules. For example, Buddhist monastic precepts have rules prohibiting sitting on fancy furniture or high chairs, or sleeping in beds raised off the floor. This works in reverse as well— even the most "fetishy" protocols and restrictions can be used as part of a spiritual discipline.

Spiritual slavery can be a path toward destruction of the "self" as the primary identity and getting past the petty demands of the ego. This is a focus of many (though certainly not all) religious traditions throughout the world, especially the ones who have a place for asceticism and meditation. Those spiritual traditions find that all their disciplines point toward one peculiar freedom. That word seems out of place when talking about slavery, but bear with me.

We live in a highly pleasure-seeking consumer culture, where individuality and freedom are too often about image and possessions rather than being able to truly define yourself as a unique individual with a meaningful life path. Freedom is often seen as the ability to act wholly for your own convenience and shallow pleasure, while meaningful choices are systematically denied to you. By choosing a simple path of obedience and discipline, by allowing all the superficial markers of individuality to be removed, you can reject that empty "freedom". Who are "you" without your stuff, your job, your social status, even your name? How can you find joy and fulfillment in doing another's will? By living this life, you *are* your unique path. In becoming this path, you render service not only to your master, but to the Universe.

Obedience to a master can parallel and model obedience to their Higher Power, as one provides inspiration and perspective for the other. It puts the focus of one's life on something external to the self, putting your personal comfort and convenience aside. In his book *Monastery: Prayer, Work, Community*, Cistercian monk M. Basil Pennington writes "Only if one leaves aside ambition—the quest for status, position, and power—can one be free to seek the will of another, to seek to walk in the way of obedience."

Raven:

Every monk needs an abbot; every nun needs an abbess. More to the point (as Joshua explores in his essay "Finding The Slow Path" later in this book), even a human being whose service is offered entirely to God or the Gods or the Universe needs some kind of human intervention to keep them on their path when it gets tough. In a spiritual M/s relationship, you do not simply give over control of your body and mind. To one extent or another (and for some it may be limited while for others it is fairly complete) you offer up your soul into the hands of the master or mistress. This requires its own kind of humility on the M-type's side.

St. Benedict gives a clear picture of this in his Rule: "The Abbot who is worthy to be over a monastery ought always to be mindful of what he is called, and make his works square with his name of 'Superior'. For he is believed to hold the place of Christ in the monastery, when he is called by his name, according to the saying of the Apostle: 'You have received the spirit of adoption of sons, whereby we cry Abba (Father)' ... Let the Abbot always bear in mind that he must give an account in the dread judgment of God of both his own teaching and of the obedience of his disciples. And let the Abbot know that whatever lack of profit the master of the house shall find in the sheep, will be laid to the blame of the shepherd. ... The Abbot ought always to remember what he is and what he is called, and to know that to whom much hath been entrusted, from him much will be required; and let him understand what a difficult and arduous task he assumeth in governing souls."

Whether or not the M-type considers themselves the s-type's spiritual superior, the s-type will still probably be coming to them for spiritual advice at least part of the time. It may not be an area that they consider to be "spiritual", but one might be surprised about that. For example, Joshua once had a weeping fit about how he couldn't join a real monastery, because he had taken vows to serve me ... and, of course, there was the little problem that he was not religiously Catholic, Buddhist, or Hindu. He didn't regret his choice; it was just the pain of commitment to a narrow path. Once you commit to something, other choices disappear. That's just life. However, the other choices still may need to be mourned.

So we talked about the monastic issue of vows of stability. That's the vow that keeps the monk from deciding that maybe that monastery over there would be better than this one, or that one, or that one—it encourages them to commit to one place and work on their stuff rather than trying to escape it by running about. Joshua came, quickly and on his own, to the realization that this was advice relevant to his commitment here—that when living a narrow, disciplined spiritual path, it is better to commit to one place and set of vows and try to work it out than to constantly obsess about all the other things you can't do.

As another example, Joshua has had problems in the past with my low-protocol approach, wishing (and sometimes nagging) that I would use more formal protocol. Remember that point we made in the last section about pride and the slave assuming that they know the "right" way to do something? It was helpful for him to read about new monks who complained that their Order was more lax than they dreamed of, and asked for more austerities to pile on them. In each case the abbot gently suggested that they get to doing the existing austerities perfectly and with a better attitude before whining for more. It's amazing how much wisdom they have for slaves.

Mindfulness

Raven:

Mindfulness is a large part of our dynamic. While we are not perfect and we don't always get it right, ideally we are aware of and scrutinize everything about our dynamic and by extension how we run the rest of our lives. I have the right to demand that Joshua tell me what he is doing, and why he thinks it's a good idea. I also have the right to veto his action, but as part of our discipline of mindfulness, it's a better thing if I simply challenge him to rethink his idea, with the addition of any information provided by my perspective. If he holds to his idea, I disagree, and I veto him, he is required to do as I ask. Then if it turns out to be a bad idea, it's on me ... and while I have the right to tell him to shut up and not point it out to me, it's better for my personal evolution for him to respectfully ask that we rethink my perspective. On the other hand, if I am doing something and he challenges me on it, I have the right to tell him that it is none of his concern—but as soon as I do that, I am then honor-bound to make sure that my ideas are sound and well thought through. As a master, although I have the right to leave him entirely out of my decision, I have the responsibility to make that decision with extra care and thought, since he is being forced to trust me entirely.

It's painfully true that a willing submissive can be made into a yes-man, but that's the worst possible thing for a dominant's evolution. Although it may be the s-type's job to make you more physically and emotionally comfortable, it's not their job to make you too *spiritually* comfortable. Nobody should ever be too spiritually comfortable, because it signifies stagnation and a lack of growth. If you're the dominant, it's on you to force yourself not to give in to the temptation of spiritual laziness while you're being pampered by the presence of your submissive.

Both parties should be asking themselves questions on a regular basis, and they should share the answers with each other. For the s-type, some questions might be: "How can I perfect my discipline of service and submission so that it improves me, not diminishes me, as a person, and serves the Divine Will through serving and submitting to this one person?" The master should be deeply involved in helping them constantly work toward this goal. On the other side, it's part of the master's responsibility to be asking critical questions like, "Does the work that I am giving this servant make good use of their abilities, or does it waste their talents and force them into work they are not well suited for? Does this work help them to become more polished in their service? Is this work set into a context that makes it easier for them to make it into a spiritual discipline? Am I respectful of their spirituality, or do I shove it aside when it inconveniences me? How am I improving myself, and could I use this dynamic and these willing hands to help me do that?"

Joshua:

When you come to the point of seeing full-time submission as a spiritual discipline, even the most fetishy protocol can aid in developing mindfulness, whether done as part of a scene or integrated into daily life. Anyone who has tried to speak in some variant of formal "slave" protocol quickly realizes that it isn't just remembering to tack a "Sir" or "Ma'am" onto the beginning and end of each statement, or mechanically replacing "I" with "this slave". For this to flow gracefully, you need to substantially modify your way of speaking, and through that, your way of thinking about yourself. For example, if you fill your conversation with "this slave wants" and "this slave has", then you are missing the point. You are still talking about yourself. A more mindful method might be to use the passive voice whenever possible—"The floor has been scrubbed" rather than "This slave scrubbed the floor." (On the other hand, this technique might be inappropriate for someone who tends to use the passive voice to avoid admitting responsibility for their errors.)

Protocols, even odd ones, can become a tool for focusing your attention. Simply crawling about on the floor, or not being able to use your hands or sit on furniture for a time shifts your perspective on how you interact with the world and the objects around you. Whether your particular D/s situation is subtle or obviously fetishy, the fact that you must think of someone else's needs and desires before your own continually refocuses you on your path. It can be something to concentrate on when the everyday struggles to obey and do a good job become overwhelming: "I'm sitting on the floor because I am a slave. My job is to obey. I chose a life where I sit on the floor, because it fulfills me. I'm going to feel the floor under my butt now, and breathe."

Sacrifice

Joshua:

There is a great satisfaction in allowing yourself, even for a brief time, to be a channel for the will of another. It gives a certain purity of consciousness that is both intoxicating and terrifying. Becoming the perfect instrument to manifest another's will is an ideal that we can never achieve, but we continue to strive for it, because the striving is the point.

However, this purity of focus sometimes requires sacrifice. For me, the sacrifice can become an act of spiritual devotion, and the submission sanctifies the service. Because this is such a narrow path, anything that gets in the way must be pruned away. This means that there are many futures that have been sacrificed. One could call it compromise—though I don't mean compromises between my master and myself. I mean situations where you want A and B, but can't have both. If you take A, does that mean not being able to take B was a sacrifice? If so, there are many sacrifices in my life. I walk a narrow path, and there are many things I feel called to that I cannot have, do, or be, because these things were sacrificed in favor of my path of service to my master. It doesn't feel right to say that *I* have made these sacrifices, because my role in the choosing is debatable, but I will say that sacrifices have been made—by my master, by Fate, by the Powers that Be, and perhaps by me as well.

Once in a while I think about the lives I might have lived if I hadn't been given to my master, and I mourn their loss. I don't regret it or resent it, but it is worth mourning occasionally. However, this is the best use of me as far as the universe is concerned, and in my heart, I know that. This type of pain is part of any life that you give yourself over to fully. I can only live one life, and it is likely that whatever life I had, I'd mourn the ones I didn't. My master told me that there is an old Romany proverb that goes, "With one butt you cannot ride two horses." Yeah, that's the way of things.

It isn't that my life in service is unfulfilling. It is incredibly fulfilling, much more so than anything I would have realistically done on my own. I was never the sort who wanted to change the world. I had no ambition; I was quite content with my place in things. I'm a cog, you know? That was fine with me. I never felt a strong desire to "make something" of myself, though for a while I thought I was terribly flawed because of that. Entering into service with my master meant that all of a sudden I was part of larger goals—his goals. This has been amazing to me. But occasionally I do miss my personal agency when it is connected to something really important to me.

Raven:

There's a lot of argument among people who play and work with D/s about whether submission is a gift that the submissive gives to the dominant. Some would agree; others would say that a slave needs to be a slave and therefore it isn't a gift, it's a necessity. For myself, I believe that my slaveboy Joshua was a gift ... from the Powers That Be, to me. He's not the one who arranged the gift, the sacrifice of himself, so it's not him that I owe. It's the Forces that gave him to me, and so I do what I understand that those Forces want me to do with my life, in return for such an amazing gift. For a while, I had a little sign on my computer terminal that said, "Josh is proof that the Gods love me and want me to be happy,"

It's his job to sacrifice so many of his desires, so much of his free will—so what's my part in return? I have my own continual self-perfecting that I work on, as does every spiritual master or mistress whom I respect. However, we are not going to be perfectly confident, perfectly organized, perfectly patient, perfectly introspective, and never erring in judgment just because we've had a slave for a few months or a year. We, too, are a work in progress, and our end-goal—should we choose to go that route—is just as difficult to achieve.

In my mind, from a spiritual perspective at least, if my slave is going to struggle to give up all his desires and values (in a very Zen-like way) and take on all of mine, then mine had better be well-scrutinized and as close to the point of perfection as I can humanly make them, in order for those values and desires to be worthy of the karma of two people. This work is my own daily sacrifice. There are many things that I'd like to do, but I'm not going to do them, because they are not worthy of my goal. He doesn't hold me to that. He couldn't. My sacrifice is to hold *myself* to it, in the face of my own desires. So there is, ideally, struggle and continual work on both sides. There will also be mistakes, procrastination, prevarication, backsliding, and general stupidity on both sides, because we are flawed humans. But that's part of the deal.

Attitude and Motivation

Joshua:

If one could find one concept that is most key to the slave's part of a spiritual relationship, it would have to be Attitude. This is both the ultimate goal and the best tool to use. The biggest spiritual struggle that a slave will have is to learn to adjust their attitude at will. If they can find the key to adjusting their attitude to be positive (or at least serene) about any situation that is thrown at them, there's nothing that they can't overcome.

It must be said that this is an ongoing process, not a goal of perfection to be reached immediately. Don't feel like a failure if you can't suddenly find a way to get a good attitude about every hard thing in your life. In, fact, beginning by focusing on the big awful things is a recipe for failure. Instead, focus on something small. Can you figure out a way to get a better attitude about this small niggling inconsequential thing? How about this one?

The most important part of the discipline of Attitude is learning that whatever you do, it is important that it be done with a whole heart. Here I'll quote the Benedictine Rule again. While I am not Christian, I found a great deal of resonance in this quote regarding Attitude:

> *This obedience, however, will be acceptable to God and agreeable to men then only if what is commanded is done without hesitation, delay, lukewarmness, grumbling or complaint, because the obedience which is rendered to Superiors is rendered to God … For if the disciple obeyeth with an ill will, and murmurs, not only with lips but also in his heart, even though he fulfill the command, it will not be acceptable to God, who regardeth the heart of the murmurer.*

When I read this, I knew exactly what he was referring to by "murmuring in the heart". I've felt that internal complaining monologue many times while my hands were obeying my master's orders. It isn't enough to simply obey, or even to obey without complaint. One must obey without resentment. This doesn't mean you have to enjoy every task (few people really enjoy cleaning the cat box, for example), but you must always try to serve without bitterness or complaint, and find what happiness in the work that you can. You must always strive to serve with an open heart, from a place of love for yourself and your master, and contentment with your role. That is more than just not whining—it means not complaining on the inside, either. It is not faking enthusiasm, but showing genuine enthusiasm and enjoying whatever work I am set to. I strive to be as naked and transparent with my master as I am before God, while being quite aware that he is not God, and not omniscient.

When we first started out, my master didn't care if I grumbled (internally or externally) when I obeyed, so long as I carried out the order. He felt that while he could reasonably order me to do things that were irritating and unpleasant (though not actually harmful), it wasn't reasonable for him to tell me not to be upset by it. My feelings weren't something that he could turn on and off like a light switch, so he allowed me my grumbling so long as I was obedient. For a while, that worked, but eventually I realized that doing my job with a bad attitude was corrosive to my soul, and to my submission. I asked him if he would be willing to require me to do better, to find ways to do even difficult work with a better mindset. He was concerned that having to "pretend" to not feel bad about doing something I disliked would make me feel even more resentful, but strangely enough, I found that it helped me to get to a place of feeling better about it.

Raven:

The master's counterpart to Attitude is Motivation. The first and most important ongoing discipline of the spiritual master is to understand their own motivations for everything they do in the relationship. Ideally, they should get to a point where every single order they give comes from a clean place. To do this requires immense self-knowledge, and then immense self-discipline. You can't figure out the motivation behind any order if you aren't brutally honest with yourself all the time. Regardless of whether you choose to inform the slave of your motivations, you should never be less than fully aware of them, and you should be able to say with certainty that they are always honorable.

Probably the most common bad motivation for an order is resentment. This happens when a master doesn't feel like they actually have the authority to change the situation—and perhaps they don't. Maybe they want to give one sort of order, but the slave has made it clear that they will resist, or otherwise be mentally unable to obey that one. They feel their authority being undermined, and a layer of seething resentment builds up. The next order comes from that place of resentment, and even if it isn't a harmful order, it will be tainted. Most slaves are very strongly attuned to their master or mistress's mental states, and they will sense that resentment, and feel unsafe. It's not good for a master to feel resentment toward their slave, because the slave is vulnerable to them—and because if they're really in charge, they can change the situation and there's no need for resentment. If there is no way that they can make any change, and the situation is so important that they can't help having serious negative emotions toward their slave, then they aren't really in charge ... of themselves *or* the slave. In that case, they need to rethink their position.

Another common bad motivation is pettiness, which is often a side effect of resentment. By definition, "pettiness" means being small inside, small and powerless. When someone is petty—and this often manifests as the act of "dicking the slave around", as my boy puts it, it strongly suggests that on some level the dominant doesn't really feel like they're in control no matter how much control they actually have, and must prove it repeatedly to their own subconscious. I should make a detour and say that it's all right to mess around with a slave's head during periods of time which are clearly labeled as play, and activities that both parties understand concretely are merely recreational. It's when the pettiness creeps outside the scene—especially when the "dicking around" pretends to be serious—that it becomes crazy-making for the slave.

On top of that, it's not spiritually good for the master either. It's especially bad when there is a hint of vengeance in the "dicking around", because vengeance implies that someone has harmed you and you have no recourse except for this striking back. If you are actually in control of your slave, they are the ones with no recourse, not you. A master who feels even a trace of the need to "get back at" their slave needs to seriously rethink the situation.

Sometimes a slave can do something that triggers a master, because we are flawed humans and we have triggers. While one would hope that we are determinedly working on those throughout our lives, M/s is emotionally serious work and emotions are often where triggers live. We get triggered, then we get angry—and the question is, do we act out of anger? There are a lot of arguments pro and con among "secular" D/s and M/s people, but our opinion is that once you step onto the road where Motivation is one of your key points, reacting from anger is never a skillful way to handle the situation. First, there's the obvious point that one's judgment is often at least a little off when one is angry. Second, reacting from anger—especially if it turns out to be a less skillful solution—can cause the slave to think twice about being honest with their less flattering emotions, and a spiritually-focused M/s relationship cannot afford even a little dishonesty. (It's all right to show your slave that they have angered you, but put that emotion somewhere else and not into an action or order.) Third, anger will often come out as defensiveness, and a master should need no defense against their slave. If they feel like they need to defend themselves, they are not in control of the slave or the situation.

Yet another common motivation is fear. This one can happen to even the most honorable master, because we all get scared sometimes. At first, it may be a fear of losing the new submissive. Later, after the relationship is well established, it may be a fear of hurting them, or of looking bad in their eyes. First we need to recognize when we are feeling fear, and perhaps take a minute before giving that panicked order. I find that using that minute just to breathe is a good way to begin.

The next step is to do whatever you need to do to step back and look at the bigger picture. After all, the big picture is our jobs, not theirs, and we as spiritual masters need to have access to that bigger picture at will. The big picture can also be comforting in its own way, especially when you are feeling lost and bogged down in overwhelming emotions. Ask yourself: *Does this order really serve the long-term goal?* Instead of coming up with answers as to why it does or doesn't, try to just clear your mind for a moment and sit with the question, and ask the Universe or whatever Holy Powers you may revere to give you the answer. If nothing comes, try breathing again. If you still don't hear anything, it's given to you to decide. Look at the long-term goal and honestly, painfully, see if the policy you were about to set really works for that goal. If it doesn't, what would work better? Don't respond from the emotions of the moment. Try to work backwards from the goal mentally—*to get X, I will need Y. To get Y, I will need Z. To get Z, I will need A. What I say next to the one under my control must support A.*

It also helps to remember that a slave who is firmly grounded in their own spirituality will be able to see the master/mistress struggling with the challenges of their own path and be proud of them, rather than thinking less of them. If the slave is caught up in their own insecurities and can't see the master's spiritual struggles as anything other than weakness, then the master needs to teach them differently. To do this right, both parties need to walk onto this path with a strong ethic of mutual honesty and appreciation for the challenges of the other person.

The master should be able to say to the slave: *It is important to me that you see me struggle with the challenges of mastery, and so long as I continue to try hard and don't give up, that you are proud of me for doing so.* The slave should be able to hear that and respond affirmatively. It's not for the sake of the master's ego—the master should not need the slave to support their ego—but for the sake of the slave being in the right place with regard to the master's flaws. In fact, the best response is, *Of course I'm proud of you, Master/Mistress. How can I help you get through this struggle?* Even if the answer is that the M-type must fight their way through it alone, it shows that the slave is seeing this as teamwork and wants to do their part, whatever that turns out to be.

Back to Motivation. Again, we can start with mindfulness. One exercise to practice this might be for the master to write down every order that they give to the slave in a one-day period—or if that seems like a lot of work, have the slave write it down for them. (Why not use the resources you have?) Then go over the list and figure out the motivation behind each one. What were you thinking and feeling when you gave that order? (This process does not have to be shared with the slave if it's still a psychologically tender issue in the early stages, unless the M-type really thinks that their slave can give them emotional support on it.) Even the simple act of teasing out a week's worth of orders can give profound insight into our characters, our needs, and the various ways in which we deceive and sabotage ourselves. This can be a great gift, because if we can't see those things, we can't change them. In the end, only half of the Discipline of Motivation is a clean order for the slave to follow. The other half is our own struggle for complete self-honesty, for knowing every inch of who we are and why we do things, and to have as much of an impact on ourselves as we do on our slaves.

That's the real trick of the Path of Mastery. While you must have initially mastered yourself in order to master another, the skillfully enacted process of mastering another can be a tool by which we further master ourselves as well.

Mastering

Raven:

A long time ago, before I had a real slave or understood any of these things I'm writing about, I was looking for a way to turn my kinky sexual practices into something spiritual, or at least a way to integrate them into what I knew was the sacredness of my own sexuality. I was lamenting to a friend about one of my fetishes, which involved certain physical objects. In a moment of divine inspiration, she pointed out that the word "fetish" had another meaning besides just some weird thing that turned you on. It could also mean a sacred object invested with holy power, which one carries to increase one's own personal spiritual power. Seen in that light, it all made sense. Of course this was a fetish—in the original sense of the word.

Mastery, too, has other meanings. To "master" someone or something is about far more than just being able to control them; it is being able to bring them to the highest possible expression of which they are capable. "Mastering" a slave may start out like "mastering" a wild horse, but the spiritual expression of that mastery should be more like "mastering" the violin, which is a process that takes years of work and patience, learning to work with the instrument rather than merely attempting to violently coerce it. If the violin is making awful noises instead of beautiful music, it isn't generally the violin's fault, and beating it isn't going to make it sound any better. The responsibility lies with the player, and their lack of skill in getting the instrument to do its best.

The word master comes from the Old English *maegester* (from which we also get "magister"), meaning "one in authority". The first part of that word, *maeg*, meant "power" in Old English. (The original Indo-European root that produced *maeg* and later *master* also produced the Sanskrit *maha*, meaning "great", as in Mahakali—Great Goddess.) *Maeg* was part of another related word—*maegen*—which referred to a particular kind of personal power. *Maegen* wasn't just self-confidence and will; it was implied that if you had enough of it—and you gained it by mindfully making commitments and keeping them, and lost it by breaking your word—when you made a formal announcement to the Universe that you were going to do something, the Universe would get behind you and push. Circumstances would line up to smooth your way.

Maegen is a formidable spiritual power, and a good description of where the master's path goes, if done rightly. After all, keeping our word and our commitments is part of the deal in base-level ethical mastery. Now add mindfulness to that. Every time you give your word on something, throw a thought in the direction of the All that says, *I want this promise written on the wall of the Universe.* When you keep it, you will gain *maegen.* (Of course, if you don't keep it, it will be disastrous, so don't do what you're not willing to follow through on.) Doing this often will create a fund of power that can be relied on when things get difficult.

So what does one do with that fund of power? Here is where we get to the difficult point. One of the requirements of spiritual mastery is that you must use the privilege of having a slave to support greater goals in your life. You don't get to use the fact that they're doing your dishes to sit around and watch *Buffy* and collect beer cans. You have to use that energy elsewhere—perhaps in a meaningful career, perhaps focusing on one's art, perhaps in doing important work in the community and the outside world. Using the practice of spiritual mastery to polish your soul and your character and to continue to make yourself a better person is also an honorable, if more internal, goal. (The essay "The Yin-Yang And The Tree" elsewhere in this book outlines how the dynamic adjusts to both internal and external Great Works.) Whatever it is, do it with your whole heart. Don't waste the gift that the Universe has given you.

So what's the next step in understanding the master's path?

Let's try the concept of honorable and sacred authority. People love and hate authority at the same time. They fear it and resent it when it is aimed in their direction, and complain when it isn't aimed fast enough at others. We have all been raised with the maxim of "power corrupts, absolute power corrupts absolutely", but those of us who practice power dynamics in our relationships cannot afford to believe that. For one thing, it means that only powerless people are good people, and that idea ought to make anyone run screaming. Beyond that, by taking power in an ethical manner and holding it in a way that is harmonious with the Universe and with the highest good for everyone involved, is a way of reclaiming power-over. We are proving that it can be done right, no matter how many times and ways it has been done wrong in the past. Power-over is the last bastion of political incorrectness, the one thing that many postmodern philosophers would claim is absolutely impossible to reclaim and make sacred—and here we are, doing it. In a way, it proves that there is nothing that cannot be cleanly reclaimed, if you are willing to work hard enough.

Perhaps the real next step is to question and possibly rework your preconceptions of the nature of leadership and authority. How have you been treated by leaders and authority figures before, in the past? If you have never had the experience of being under someone competent whom you respected, and if all your experiences of authority have been perceived as corrupt and abusive, you are at a disadvantage when it comes to doing it correctly yourself. It might be worth it to look for good role models, and not necessarily in the BDSM demographic (although if you find them easily there, it's fine). Even reading about honorable leaders and analyzing their style might work for you—what made them honorable? What burdens did they face that might have tempted them to be less so? Did they make mistakes, and how did they handle that? Also, learn about yourself. Delve into yourself and find the unconscious triggers that can trick you into doing things for the wrong reasons. To be a spiritual dominant is to engage in constant soul-searching.

The next step is to develop a strict code of honor. It should be designed to force you to be ethical to those around you, not to protect your pride from the pain of having to question your motives. Give some thought to what will happen if some external damage renders you unable to treat those close to you safely and ethically.

Your submissive should be able to trust you with their life, their body, their soul, and their sanity, and know that you treat them with their well-being in mind, even while you ask them to sacrifice some amount of comfort and convenience for you.

My own code of honor is bound up with the concept of *noblesse oblige*. This translates roughly to "the obligations of the nobility". Since my youth, I've always been unable to shake the idea that I am a superior person. I know all the reasons people would tell me that this is a wrong attitude, and I've tried them on intellectually, but deep down underneath, I just can't stop believing it unless I load myself with a crippling amount of self-hatred, which can't be the answer to anything good. So, as part of my personal discipline of redeeming anything that could be construed as an "evil", I adhere to the code of *noblesse oblige*. This states that if I really believe that I am a superior human being, I'd better act like one. That doesn't mean acting like a supercilious jerk. It means having a discipline of courtesy to all people at all times, no matter what. It means acting noble, for real, without exception, even in the face of rudeness and exhaustion and difficulty. If I'm really a superior human being, I should be able to pull that off. This puts my personal "delusion" squarely in the service of my own personal growth.

Joshua:

During the period when I was looking for a service relationship, I did a great deal of thinking about makes someone worthy to be a servant, but not much about what makes someone worthy of serving. I had fallen heavily into the "pure service" mindset where it doesn't matter if the master or mistress is worthy; so long as they aren't openly harmful to their slaves, any hardship can theoretically be turned into a field for spiritual work. In much BDSM pornography, the first big criteria for owning a slave seems to be wealth (and occasionally a big cock), and slaves are supposed to find fulfillment in the act of pure service itself, even if they are serving unpleasant or immoral people.

The second big dominance criteria in porn is the master's ability to maintain unfailing control through constant displays of strength and superiority. Some people on power-dynamic Internet forums worry about what would happen if the master/mistress becomes ill and can no longer keep their slave "in line". This is entirely contrary to my idea of how these relationships work. Being a good slave means that you provide service in times of strength and of weakness. You are serving a fallible and human person. If you cannot care for your master after his stroke, push his wheelchair, and consider him no less your master, you have utterly failed him and failed yourself.

This is a crucial part of spiritual surrender. It is reasonable to be able to expect your master to hold to their part of the "bargain" when that involves ethical behavior, honor, self-awareness, guidance, good judgment, and general maturity. It is not reasonable to expect an eternal and unchanging supply of youth, good health, sexual energy, and continual "dominant persona". If nothing else, we all get old (if we don't die first) and it would be nice to assume that this relationship would continue well into old age, and that the dynamic would still find a way to survive without fetishistic trappings.

Each s-type will decide for themselves what makes an M-type worth serving, and it is important to hold out for high standards, but it's also important to see them as human and be all right with that. It's frustrating sometimes, because we often secretly want our M-types to be as perfect as possible, and when they continually forget to flush the toilet or leave the cap off the toothpaste or refuse to stop and ask for directions, it's hard not to become angry and resentful.

However, masters are human, and part of the spiritual path of being a slave is the great leap of courage and faith that it takes to be willing to serve that imperfect human being. If it is the will of the Universe, or God, or however you see it, that you serve this person right here in front of you—the one with all those faults—then your job is to do that to the best of your ability. This should include learning to find ways to cope with their imperfections, and not let those imperfections stop you from doing your own job. Your first line of defense is to find a way to get right with where they are and what they ask of you—and you can ask for their help in this task, and a good master will give it to you. Only when that course of action has utterly failed do you look for more extreme solutions.

Masters and Society

Raven:

At this point in time—the year 2011—when we speak to groups of people about spiritual M/s, some of the most frequent questions that we get are from submissives and would-be slaves who are searching for a spiritual dominant and can't find one, or who are interviewing with putatively spiritual dominants, and would really prefer finding one who was further along their spiritual path than the would-be slave. Sometimes these issues come up when we are counseling couples in their relationship. These two similar problems seem to come from a general lack of masters and would-be masters who are pursuing this path, in comparison to the numbers of would-be slaves. While this is all anecdotal and we certainly have no statistics, it does seem that fewer M-types than s-types actively desire this kind of path. In other words, everywhere in America that we travel, there seems to be a shortage of spiritually-focused masters.

There could be a number of explanations for this—including the possibility of a skewed demographic, as there is some evidence that there are fewer M-types than s-types overall—but one possible explanation for this is that the very nature of submission can force you into a transcendent, ego-destroying spiritual place you didn't expect, whereas the mastery path requires more active pursuing and solitary struggle. One doesn't inadvertently fall into it; it requires constant work. There's also a lot less information about it out there, and dominants are less willing to talk about their sensitive issues in public, leaving newer dominants with no signposts. This means that until the numbers even out, there are going to be a lot more s-types in this predicament.

Also—and this too is just what we've seen—while the spiritual path of service and submission can make it easier for a sub or slave to adapt to their situation—this does not seem to be true for the path of spiritual mastery. It can make our situations deeper, more meaningful, more honorable, more in tune with the Universe, more self-aware, and generally more rewarding—but not any easier. In fact, sometimes it seems to make things harder. I can see why this would put off the majority of dominants, and thus create the apparent disparity that has so many s-types bemoaning the lack of an appropriate spiritual dominant.

But there's yet another reason that no one is talking about. Recently an s-type was bemoaning this problem, and in doing so enumerated all the great spiritually progressive qualities that she wanted in a dominant. "Where are all the masters who have those qualities?" she was saying, in essence.

I know where they are. They're where I was for so many years— wrapped up in spiritual communities that tell them, over and over, that the kind of relationship they're in is not ethically acceptable, much less a spiritual possibility. I spent years in progressive spirituality communities of various sorts, and I still speak at a lot of spiritual and religious gatherings, although no longer any of the New Age/meditative/political/nonviolence variety. I know those cultures. I know the enormous pressure in those spiritual subcultures to be militantly egalitarian, to see taking any power over your partner as absolutely unacceptable. Which means that 90% of the kind of people that spiritual s-types are seeking are over in those subcultures, being spiritual and getting it pounded into them at every turn that D/s is Not OK and that there is no healthy way to do it, that it will inevitably lead to abuse and corruption. Of course they aren't advertising!

If their desires do lead them into the BDSM demographic, they tend to keep it Only Play; owning another person is still Not OK. It takes a huge leap away from everything that they've been taught, and that the progressive spiritual leaders who they respect have told them is evil. And I see lots of complaining about there not being enough spiritual masters on this side of the line, but I see no one trying to help the problem from the other side of the line. I don't see submissives doing presentations in sex-positive spiritual groups over there about "This is why we want to live this way, this is why it isn't evil, and this is the high standard of spiritual dominant that we seek." I don't see spiritual dominants giving presentations to crystalhuggers about how it is possible to own another person and still be a sensitive, honorable, spiritual person. I don't see either group being willing to take the decade or so of virulent flak that they will get from frightened people in those subcultures, until it changes. *But if no one does it, nothing is going to change over here on this side of the line.*

Joshua and I have spent the last decade presenting on spiritual D/s to our faith community, which is fairly progressive and has an overlap with the above subcultures. We've finally gotten to the point where we can present on this at national conferences in our faith. At the same time, I get hate mail and the occasional death threat. But we've made changes, and it can be done with time and perseverance. (The fact that we are both guys has helped. If either of us was a woman, it would be much harder. But someone needs to go that route too, after us.)

So I challenge the submissives who are looking and complaining: Look to the communities where people learn to be spiritual in the way that you prefer. What can be done to make it acceptable to also be dominant (or submissive, subs often take heat there too) in those ideologies? What can *you* do about that? (And I'm challenging the dominants over here as well.)

Joshua:

I think it is especially hard for many heterosexual submissive women (and that's who I hear complaining the most) to understand that extremely few of the sensitive, loving, spiritually-clued-in heterosexual men out there are ever going to find themselves in circumstances that encourage them to explore a desire for sexual domination in a healthy way. That is so entirely unacceptable for them on so many levels. It is a really rare and unique guy who finds both of those things in his life. This means that the het scene is strongly biased towards not-so-spiritual, not-so sensitive guys.

Dominant women may also turn toward a spiritual path that eschews inegalitarian relationships, especially if they fear being forced by society to be submissive, and they don't trust any group or system not to backtrack into that cultural pattern. The current aesthetic in the BDSM demographic about how dominant women are supposed to act, look, and run their relationships is often a serious turnoff for thoughtful and spiritually aware women who just like to be in charge. One of the big complaints we've heard is about the idea that dominant women paired with submissive men have to withhold sex in order to keep their power, and are not emotionally intimate with their s-types. In addition, trusting men to submit mindfully may take a giant leap of faith for them.

As we mention frequently in our sections of this book, spirituality is a force that tends to overflow any container you put it in. That's how you know it's real. When strongly spiritual people are forced to choose between their path—or the best approximation of it they can find at the moment—and their sexuality, they tend to choose their path, even if it means cutting off that part of themselves. So they may gravitate to the spiritual culture, have egalitarian relationships (although perhaps not without a certain amount of power struggle), and live their lives distrusting power dynamics. If we don't give them examples that make sense and that they can relate to, they'll stay over there. Many of these individuals have put a lot of time into learning relationship skills and striving for better intimacy. The current cultural emphasis of the BDSM demographic on a mode of behavior for dominants that is distant and sinister, however titillating that might be for people in the scene, tends to look less than mature to them.

That Thing Called Religion

Raven:

When you get a bunch of people together talking about how they apply spirituality to a specific activity, you often get a lot of differentiating between "spirituality" and "religion". It's not uncommon for half the people to have a unilaterally positive opinion of "spirituality" and shove all the negative qualities into the "religion" category, especially if they have wounding and damage from early experiences with religious organizations. However, we are going to be a little more objective about these terms. For the purposes of this section of the book, the main difference between these terms is that "spirituality" refers to a solely personal path which need not share symbols, theories, or make any sense at all to anyone else, while "religion" is "spirituality" which is a group practice, and must share some commonality of ideas and symbols or it won't function as such.

We can't discuss this broad subject without making a detour into the territory of religion, because at least some M/s couples who are working toward this practice actually do have established faiths. While religions often differ so much that it may be impossible to make a blanket statement about them, we can safely say that from the outside, the first big question that people ask when putting the words "slave" and "religion" in the same sentence is about religious freedom. They want to know whether the concept of religious freedom (which is one of the founding concepts of the country I live in, at any rate) applies to a slave who might theoretically have no freedom. Do masters ever force a slave to convert to a religion, or at least to go through the motions? Do they prevent a slave from practicing their own faith? Do they attempt to condition a slave into holding the same religious beliefs as they do? Even if the majority of M/s couples might scoff at the idea, it's worth discussing if only for the sake of the curious who might be reading this book, and having those uncomfortable thoughts come up in the back of their minds.

I won't say that the first situation has never happened. However, I'll say about that what I would say about any M/s situation where someone is unhappy with what is being asked of them: these are subjects that should be worked out clearly in the beginning negotiations. If it is very important to the dominant that the submissive share their faith, it would be best for them to seek only within their faith group. If it is very important to the s-type to be allowed to practice their religion, then they should choose a dominant who is fine with that, along with their stance on other sticky subjects like money, polyamory, and keeping one's career. Put it on the list of interview questions and don't settle for less.

There may be certain situations where the dominant is tied to their religious faith more for cultural and social reasons than because of a deeply held faith relationship, and it's important for their partner to be willing to share that culture and be seen as belonging to that society. In that case, the dominant may not care very much if the submissive is just going through the motions, so long as the motions are correct. There are also certain religious groups who believe that "going through the motions will eventually lead to a faith conversion experience". I could see how a master from one of those groups might hope to make an "infidel" slave convert, but personally I would consider that a long shot and suggest, again, that there would be less chance for disappointment in choosing from one's own faith group. A religious conversion is not, in my experience, something that can be ordered, or even coaxed and cajoled. It comes or it doesn't, because in any dealings with the numinous, it is the numinous that decides who is called and for what, not the human beings on the ground at the time.

The problem usually comes in when the slave is very devout. It's the same issue regardless of whether the owner is very devout in another faith, or a complete atheist: can they respect the slave's religious beliefs, even when those beliefs are inconvenient to the owner? Each master/mistress will have to work out for themselves what's too much. Differences can arise from religiously-based ethical beliefs clashing, or the need for particular observances becoming inconvenient, time-consuming, and/or expensive. I've definitely seen situations where the master was vaguely contemptuous of the slave's religious beliefs, or at least fairly dismissive, but as long as the religious practices didn't "interfere"—meaning as long as they didn't trespass onto the master's convenience—it was allowed in the same way that they might allow any other silly but harmless little hobby.

However, as soon as those religious beliefs became too visible or got in the way of the slave obeying a conflicting order, it wasn't "harmless" any more and something had to be done about it. What was done depended on the strength of the slave's beliefs. Some were willing to drop their beliefs, or at least keep their practice in the closet in order to please their masters. Some weren't willing to compromise, and left. Religion is, all too often, one of those issues where everyone hopes that if they just ignore the differences, they won't matter, when actually making them not matter requires communication, mutual respect, and work, not willful blindness on the matter.

For myself, I believe that God(s) trump masters, so I would find it hypocritical and spiritually wrong to cut someone off from their religion. As someone who believes that abandoning a clear spiritual path for short-sighted reasons can have real-life negative repercussions, I'd also consider it somewhat dangerous. I was once told of such a situation by one member of a couple, and I have never forgotten the story. They were in a M/f power dynamic. He was a practitioner of Islam. She was raised in an Afro-Caribbean faith, and dedicated to Yemaya the Ocean Mother, goddess of home and childbirth, in her teens. Her parents acknowledged her desire to have children, but asked Yemaya to help her hold off until she was an adult in a financially stable situation. At first her master allowed her to practice her faith, but after a few years and a few children, he cracked down and told her to get rid of her altar and stop practicing. Within months, they were homeless and their children had been removed by the authorities. It was not until after she reinstated her altar and her practice—rebelling against his orders—that they were able to find housing and get their children back. What Yemaya had so graciously given was promptly taken away. From a less polytheistic stance, the desires of a partner—even one who supposedly owns you—are not as important to the Universe as following one's own dedicated path. In my worldview, since he was the one in charge, taking away her beloved spiritual practice for reasons having nothing to do with her own good, only his own discomfort, was not good spiritual mastery.

Of course, there is the question as to whether the submissive is actually devout or just holding to conditioned beliefs for cultural reasons. Do they believe that X is an integral part of their spiritual beliefs, or were they just taught by their parents or church that X is what good (insert denomination here) followers do? If it's the latter—if they are following an unquestioned cultural belief rather than defending a cornerstone of the foundation of their belief—and the dominant deeply believes that their mutual faith need not be interpreted by those cultural rules, then that's a different war. I would then support the dominant's efforts to show the submissive that they could live their faith without those cultural trappings. I might also support a dominant who felt that a particular belief was actively harmful to their submissive's health or self-worth, and wanted to work on changing that, out of direct concern for their submissive's well-being, but that's a touchy area. I might suggest that the best way for the dominant to do this cleanly is to have the submissive talk to others who fought that battle and made it out the other side. For example, if a submissive was tormenting themselves about certain of their sexual desires being spiritually wrong, and the dominant not only felt that they were not wrong, but believed that attitude to be harming the submissive's self-esteem, they might find it most effective to have theirs submissive listen to people in their faith who came to a place of spiritual peace and acceptance with those desires.

But, basically, it comes down to this for a slave who is caught between a religious belief and their master's orders: are you more afraid of defying your Higher Power and your spiritual path, or defying your master? If you're in the former category, you'll defy your master and hold to your beliefs, no matter what—and your Higher Power will give you that strength, no matter how owned you are, even breaking the master's hold on you if necessary. If you're more afraid of your dominant than you are of God, then you're not really all that religious.

Joshua:

When the master and slave share the same religious worldview and have compatible practices, integrating these things into their relationship tends to go fairly smoothly, and the inevitable struggles tend to bring both people deeper into their faith and deeper into their relationship. But when their beliefs or practices are not so compatible, the resulting struggles are likely to put one or both people in a very difficult position.

If the master devoutly practices a particular religion or spiritual path, and the slave is largely indifferent to such things, I think it is entirely reasonable for the master to expect the slave to follow the basic tenets and prohibitions of the master's religion. Insisting the slave adopt certain beliefs may be beyond the master's ability (if not beyond their authority), but I think a slave is unlikely to be harmed by having to engage in religious practices they are not particularly enthusiastic about. (For example, there is absolutely no harm in a non-Jewish slave being required to keep a kosher kitchen.) Religions generally offer clear guidance on the extent to which non-believers (including spouses of believers) may participate in their religious ceremonies. Certainly they can be expected to not violate the rules of conduct specified by their master's religion, especially if those rules of conduct are believed to be appropriate for all people to follow, rather than specific to practitioners of this religion. Religious traditions generally offer ample guidance as to when exceptions are appropriate—such as whether it is required to fast when pregnant, or if it is permissible to lie if it will save someone's life.

However, if the master wants the slave to formally convert to a particular religion, I would recommend both parties get counsel from a reputable leader in their religious community. The master/slave issue need not be discussed; only the issue of whether it is appropriate for a person to formally convert prior to establishing a deep connection to that religion. In some religious traditions, conversion is seen primarily as membership in a spiritual community, not a profession of faith or a life-long commitment. In others, conversion is a serious promise to believe in and uphold the tenets of this faith, perhaps not just in this lifetime, but beyond it.

If the slave has an attachment of some kind to a different religious tradition than the master's, things become more challenging. The first thing to consider is what the general stance is in the master's religious tradition towards the slave's religious tradition. Some traditions "agree to disagree", while others believe that any tradition which doesn't agree with certain basic tenets is fundamentally wrong and dangerous. The latter situation makes it incredibly hard to maintain a spiritually-focused power dynamic if the people involved are deeply committed to opposing traditions. (Of course, one hopes that a fundamental difference that deep would have been sorted out in the negotiation stage, and would probably be an initial deal-breaker for most people.)

If the two religious traditions are reasonably tolerant of each other and in agreement on most key issues, differences in practice may not cause much of a problem, but be aware that even small differences can become a big source of conflict. For instance, the distinction between tithing and love offerings might seem trivial, until money becomes tight and the slave wants to contribute more to their church than the master thinks is necessary. Whether or not your power dynamic resembles a marriage, the advice given to people in "mixed marriages" is often helpful, even if the compromises tend to all go in one direction.

We frequently meet couples where the slave is very devout, and the master is either an atheist or simply much less invested in any particular religion. As Raven said, this often results in the master treating the slave's religion like a hobby, tolerating it so long as it doesn't become inconvenient. (The tendency for slaves to be religious more often than masters may have something to do with the fact that many masters consider religion to be just another thing that tries to tell them what to do, and they won't stand for that.) When it does become inconvenient, the master—often having limited understanding of the slave's religious practices—may make decisions that put the slave in a very difficult position, and may seriously damage the trust built between them.

I'd like to suggest masters take a more proactive approach, especially if the slave is at all devout or expects the master to make any allowances whatsoever for their religious beliefs or practices. First, learn a bit about the slave's religion, so you understand the basic context of the practices. Second, talk with the slave about their religion, especially the practices and beliefs which affect daily life and decision making. If there are certain rules or guidelines that they live by because of their religion, get them spelled out clearly in a way that makes sense to you. Talk about realistic hypothetical scenarios until you are confident that you can understand the way that these rules are actually applied in daily life. Many religions share the same basic rules, but interpret them very differently. For example, does a religious prohibition on killing forbid killing in self-defense or military action? Does it forbid eating meat?

Next, talk to your slave about their religion's stance on obedience and submission. Is there a spiritual context for recognizing one person having lawful spiritual authority over another? Do they think that this relationship qualifies? Do they have a spiritual obligation to obey you? Under what circumstances would that obligation to obey override their obligation to follow certain spiritual rules? Does it matter whether they are breaking a spiritual rule by action versus breaking it by inaction? Does it matter whether it was intentional or unintentional? What are the spiritual consequences for disobedience, either to established spiritual rules or to the orders of a spiritual superior? What is the spiritually correct course of action for a person to take after some wrongdoing? What are the spiritual consequences for wrongdoing? Questions such as these give you insight into the slave's inner life, and also provide ideas on how to use the slave's religious beliefs to motivate their obedience and submission.

Then, find someone the slave respects in their religious tradition who can offer you advice and information. The slave's clergyperson is generally a good choice, but the ideal is to find someone in their religious community whose judgment they would defer to in spiritual matters, even if it differed sharply from their own. (If the slave is more "spiritual" than "religious", it is still reasonable for the master to ask the slave to find them a disinterested third party with similar beliefs or practices, who can provide some perspective on the slave's spiritually-based decisions.) If any of the rules your slave described are problematic to you, ask this person for a second opinion on their spiritual necessity, and under what circumstances exceptions would be generally deemed acceptable. If appropriate, ask about issues of submitting to lawful authority, obedience, and consequences for wrongdoing. Ask if there are any other important rules or guidelines for behavior that your slave didn't mention.

Finally, talk to your slave about what you've learned, and what conclusions you've come to thus far. Encourage them to express any concerns they have. Make it clear that spiritually-based objections will be taken seriously, but not automatically accepted. It is fine to put practical limits on how much time, physical space, and money the slave can devote to their various spiritual practices. ("No, you can't run away on a mission to the Congo.") It is fine to confront the slave if their spiritual practices seem detrimental or self-serving.

If the master finds aspects of the slave's religion that strongly reinforce the power dynamic, it can be very beneficial to insist the slave deeply explore those aspects. I think it is entirely reasonable for a master to insist that a slave follow any of the tenets of the slave's own religion more closely than the slave might be inclined to, especially if the master is being inconvenienced by some of the slave's other religious practices.

Sacred Power

Of Mastery And Service

Lee Harrington

(Originally published in Sacred Kink: The Eightfold Paths of BDSM)

Having someone at my feet moaning my honorific can indeed be an aphrodisiac, but Mastery as a spiritual calling, as a vocation, has so much more potential for me to grow, learn, evolve, and serve the Universe. Sometimes, I think of this in the context of the Sanskrit term *guru*. Though meaning "teacher", or "individual with great knowledge in an area", its folkloric translation is "destroyer of darkness." Following the calling of Mastery I provide myself as teacher, as guide, as icon, as mentor, as authority. In doing so, from a place of authenticity and integrity, I become a guru. I am gifted with the ability to clear the darkness and find the truths buried within.

In Mastery, we do not strive for Mastery of any one person, but of ourselves. How can we possibly hope to guide another life if we ourselves have not taken the time to learn to guide our own lives? Until we are rich in spirit and strongly rooted in knowledge of our own journey, we are only donning the guise of Mastery.

This work is ever-evolving. This work is never done. This work of self-mastery involves learning honesty with ourselves. Involves coming from the heart. Involves questing for our greatness. Involves living in integrity. Involves constant self-examination. Involves finding our head, heart, and cunt/cock in full alignment. Thus, with each day we do this work we are in obedience to our call of Mastery, whether we have a Slave or not.

When the gift of service comes to us, how do we give thanks? If someone has come into my life to do part of my work, leaving my hands open, I am called to apply my open hands to the great work. To my life's Work. To do something bigger with myself. It is not a question of "what have I done to deserve this gift?" but "what will I keep doing to continue to be worthy of this gift?"

Thus, Mastery is also a path of spiritual submission. I am called to stretch the boundaries of my greatness and potential not through ego, but through surrender. Mastery is a form of service, to the universe, to ourselves, to those we are in charge of. Giving and receiving service is a dance. The service that I give may have no resemblance on the surface to the service my Slave gives me, but they are both serving a greater good.

For me to excel in what I give the Universe in my service, I must learn to accept service with grace. Each bow holds power, each load carried, each dish done. Their acts enable me to move forward with greatness. And how we treat those under us often determines how the Universe will treat us in turn.

Our Place And Our Path
Lady Rafaella

I. Pathia

Years ago, I named my slave girl Pathia. At the time, I thought that it was just a pretty word, but later I found out that it is a feminized form of the Greek-derived suffix *path*, which means both to suffer from something and to practice it. (Like *neuropathy* and *osteopathy*.) We both found this to be perfect, because that's what consensual slavery is for her: a way of turning what would otherwise be suffering into a spiritual practice. That's the way our relationship works. An inspiration will come, and we'll think it's something ordinary until we discover that it's not. It's another message, another gateway that leads us further down the road together.

Pathia and I have been together for eight years. We met at a lesbian softball game, where we were both out of place. I saw this beautiful girl with a lovely tattoo on the side of her shaved head, and I spent the next hour angling around to get a glimpse of it. Finally she caught me looking and called out, "If you want to come look at it, who don't you come over here?" So I did, and we ended up blowing off the game to go on an impromptu date at a café, which led to my apartment and a night of long talking. There wasn't any sex that night because I was sleeping on the couch in the common room (a recent ex-lover was occupying my bedroom, promising to be out any day now), but there was immediate chemistry.

She was a submissive and I was a fairly new dominant. We'd both had bad experiences—her with crazy, bitchy dominant women who used their position to excuse petty irrational behavior, and me with crazy, whiny subs who would act out and want to be treated like children. We bonded over the concept of a D/s relationship being an agreement between two adults who promise to hold to the rules even when they might be difficult, and who actually keep their promises. I wanted a powerful servant, not a child with no self-control. She wanted a powerful Lady who held to a code of honor.

By the time we sleepily showered and left for work at dawn, we knew that we'd both found what we were looking for.

That was how we began, and I really think that beginning set the scene for where we would go together. Making dominance and submission into a spiritual path isn't for everyone. It's advanced work. You both have to be grownups first. This isn't for immature people who are using D/s as a way to avoid learning relationship skills, or for immature dominants who want someone to shore up their pathetic egos, or immature submissives who want someone to control them because they can't control themselves. It has to start with two people who are adult enough to hold to a discipline, because discipline is what it will be for both people.

The next night—after I had come home from work and gotten some sleep—I took out my deck of Tarot cards and did a reading. I've been reading Tarot as a spiritual practice, kind of a way of praying to God and asking Him for advice, since I was a teenager. The cards showed me as a knight on a white horse, going on a quest ... but then they torpedoed the idea that the quest was meant to rescue or save Pathia. She was not to be my damsel in distress. She was meant to be my support, on the big Quest, to serve me.

I didn't understand. At the time I was a social worker in a dead-end job that I hated, and there was little to no higher meaning in my life outside of my Tarot practice. The next day I was awakened by a call from a friend who was offering me a job. A big job—coordinating a private shelter for abused women. It would mean a whole lot of extra hours for not much more pay. It would be emotionally grueling. It terrified me, and I knew that there was no way I could turn it down. I called Pathia and told her about it, even though I barely knew her and I had no idea how she'd react, especially when I mentioned the part about having a lot less time to date and party. That was hard to say to the person I'd just started dating, but she was just silent for a moment and then said, "I'll support you in any way that I can, my Lady."

That's when I knew that this had all been arranged. God was looking out for me. He always does.

II. The Problem of Religion

Two weeks later she knelt to me under the moon in a park at night. We'd scouted around the make sure that there were no prowlers ready to harass two women alone, but we were both armed just in case. It seemed appropriate, anyway. She laid her big folding knife at my feet and pledged her service to me, and I accepted it as her liege lady. We swore to be honest and honorable with each other always, even when it was hardest. I put a chain around her neck and locked it, but gave her the key because she had to take it off to go to work. Eventually the chain became a necklace that doesn't come off, but that was later.

She had to go away on a family trip, so we spent the time apart working out how we wanted the relationship to go, over email. I started my new job and it was just as nerve-wracking and as rewarding as I'd expected it to be. I also gritted my teeth and did the hardest thing of all—I talked to Pathia about my spiritual beliefs. I was raised Christian, and I went through at least five different denominations ending with MCC, but even though I wasn't attending any churches at the moment I still considered myself somehow Christian ... if a weird, strange Christian whose main method of prayer was Tarot cards. I knew that she had been a radical, a street punk, and that in my experience those people tended to scorn anything remotely like religion or even spirituality, and I feared her believing that her new Mistress was deluded. In hindsight, I should have shared that before our whirlwind collaring, but I was so caught up in my feelings that I missed the obvious.

I was right, and Pathia was a staunch atheist. She was a little bewildered, but felt better when I reassured her that I wasn't going to try to convert her and that I wouldn't force her to come to church with me if I decided to attend again. I tried to explain it to her that my God was my dominant, but I'd been smart and chosen the compassionate and loving one and not the hateful and vengeful one. With sudden inspiration, I added that she could think of all the Christian hatemongers as submissives who had signed up with a bad dominant because of their damage, or because they didn't do their due diligence in choosing one, or because they couldn't bear to leave the abusive one they'd grown up, with even if it was bad for them.

Pathia told me later that with that one conversation, I blew her mind and completely changed the way that she thought about religion and religious fanatics. A month later, she found herself looking at the guy harassing people with nasty hate-filled tracts on the subway and thought, "I've got a good dominant, and my dominant has a good dominant, but you've got a bad dominant who makes you do awful things." She felt pity instead of anger, which was at least a step in the right direction.

A couple of years into our relationship, after she had moved in with me, Pathia came to me and confessed that she had been having thoughts about her own spiritual path, but she had been worried about talking to me because she wasn't drawn to Christianity. She had read the Benedictine Rule and found that it resonated with her, but the words "monk" and "nun" still made her recoil because she associated them with celibacy, and kinky sex was so much a part of our relationship. She was starting to be drawn to some of the Eastern faiths and wanted my blessing to explore them. I gave it, of course, and she embarked on a "seeking" phase, trying out Buddhism and Hinduism and a few others. After about a year of this, she came back to me and said out of nowhere, "I want to be your slave, and I want that to be my religion."

Up until then, we had been dominant and submissive instead of mistress and slave, but that changed soon after. First, though, I had to stop blinking in surprise and find out what she meant by her religion being living as my slave. Was I supposed to be her god? I wasn't comfortable with that, even though all the references to "worship" in BDSM seemed to be about sex, not real worship. But that wasn't what she wanted, either. She put something together for herself that is half eastern religions and half ... well, doing slave things with mindfulness of why she was doing them, and giving them deeper meaning. Even after she became my slave, I did not become her goddess. I became the focus through which she renders service to the Universe, but I am the doorway, not what is beyond it.

III. In Your Place

We use the words "in your place" a lot in our relationship. Those words have some pretty negative connotations in society, because it seems like they're always used to keep people in places they don't want to be in. For us, the connotation is different. When Pathia is "in her place" it means that she knows who and what she is and is not ashamed of it—it's just the way things should be. It means that she is comfortable with being my servant. She often feels guilty about being submissive, because she was taught that it was extra important for women to be ambitious and independent, and she gets caught between wanting to be what society needs and what she really is. I tell her that I have enough ambition and independence for five women, so I can not only absorb hers but provide enough to absorb three other slave girls, should it come to that. (Which it won't, as I have decided that we are monogamous for now.) This sounds silly but it makes her feel a lot better.

Pathia and I have decided that it is her place to serve me and to do as I say with her life, and that it is my place to direct her mind, body, heart, and soul. She came to this decision through exploring what made her feel most comfortable with her life and herself. I came to this decision through prayer and divination. We are unanimous on what should be done. The struggle is all in how to do it best. I'm still learning this lesson.

I'm not a perfect Mistress. I wish I was better at so many things. When I make a mistake with Pathia—or even, sometimes, in front of her—I feel like I've let her and our relationship down. Since I'm human, I'm doomed to make mistakes, and since she is my servant and lives her life at my heel, she's doomed to see every one of them up close. But I serve a God of love and mercy, and He forgives me when I err and inspires me to keep trying.

I did eventually notice that sometimes I would make a tiny mistake, and she would become upset with me and think that I wasn't competent to be her mistress. Other days, I would make a slightly bigger error and she would be fine with my flawed humanity. We discussed it and watched for the different responses, and it turned out that it was less about whatever error I'd made and more about whether she was in her place. Now when she is feeling upset because I forgot to pick up the takeout, I tell her to do what she needs to do to get back into her place. That might be to meditate, or to go outside and take a walk and think, or to just lay on the floor at my feet for a while. (This last one helps to give her a very physical lesson about where her place is. Sometimes she will come to me and ask to just lay at my feet in order to get back into her place.)

IV. Spiritual Skills

Our path has come around to me being her spiritual superior, although I was uncomfortable with that as well, in the beginning. How could I be the spiritual superior of someone in a different faith than myself? But over time I began to see two truths: first, that we are on the same path in this relationship, and second, that I had collected many spiritual skills over time that she was just beginning to understand. I know that prayer—or meditation, or being with nature, or the other things that quiet the soul—are useful even, and perhaps especially, when one is upset and unbalanced. I know that no matter how strong your faith, there will be times when you will be furious with God or the universe. I know that this is normal and that there are ways through it. I know that a job done with resentment is poisonous to the soul. These and many other spiritual skills are where I am mentoring her as her spiritual superior.

At the same time, I help her to make her service to me more perfect. For example, she volunteers at the women's shelter where I work. At first she did this so that we could spend more time together during the day, but now she has become my assistant there as well. Since we have to be low-key there, we have worked out special protocols for her that help both her spiritual well-being and my comfort. In the morning, a cup of coffee and a healthy snack will be waiting for me after I have the morning check-in with my staff. This keeps me from wandering into the kitchen where there is tempting junk food that I'm trying to avoid. As Pathia prepares it and leaves it on my desk, she says what I would call a prayer and what she prefers to call an affirmation—that her Mistress will be alert and well-nourished. She says the same prayer over lunch and over dinner. These and other small protocols help to keep her focused on her job of sacred service.

I used to worry that what I do with a deck of Tarot cards was somehow spiritually wrong, because of all the assumptions of some Christians that all such things are of the Devil, or at least are "cheating God". I don't believe in the Devil, but I did worry about cheating God until I went to a reading with a shaman. (When I'm not clear-headed and the gift doesn't work, the best thing I can do is to go for a second opinion with a skilled reader who is neutral to the situation.) I admitted my worry, and he told me that it was foolish, because the idea that we could cheat God is foolish, and an act of hubris. He told me that he was sure that the Holy Powers (as he called them) could easily stop the gift at any moment if there was a good reason. He also told me that he had often run into a deliberate wall not of his making when reading for some people, and he was quite certain that this was because it would mean more to them if they figured it out on their own. The gift was a tool given to us by the Holy Powers, he told me, and to refuse it would be as silly as refusing any other gift we were given.

So once a week I sit down and light a candle—my "Pathia" candle, which is a red one that she gave me for a gift and that I have rubbed with her sexual fluids—and I pray to God to tell me how Pathia is doing inside, how I can better help her on her path, how I am doing with my own path, and what I can work on to be a better master over the next week. Then I deal four cards in a square for each of these questions, and a fifth one in the middle for "Is there anything else You think I should know, God?" Sometimes the answers are hard. Sometimes they make me cringe, like when the cards say that I need to be more organized and procrastinate less, because it sets a good example for Pathia and will make her feel more secure. Sometimes I can't understand the reading. When that happens, I try to remember the shaman's advice and I assume that I need to figure it out on my own. Once in a while something will happen later in the week and I'll realize what was meant by the reading, which helps me to see patterns when that comes up again.

A turning point came for me when my Tarot cards were ruined in a plumbing flood. I'd been using the same old deck for years, even though its artwork wasn't quite right for me. I'd seen some beautiful decks in stores, but I'd refrained from buying them because some part of me was still compartmentalizing my Tarot practice away from my faith. I didn't know whether this was a sign from God that I should stop, or that I should do something else. Then Pathia hesitantly brought out two Tarot decks that she had bought for me on impulse as a surprise, but then hidden in a closet because she didn't know if I would want them. She had picked both because they had beautiful Christian iconography, and I knew that accepting them would mean accepting integrating the two sides of my practice. Sometimes God chooses to guide one through one's slave, too.

Five cards from the old deck survived the flood, the five that had been on top when I had read them last. Two were our "significators", meaning the cards that we associate with ourselves: the Queen and the Page of Wands. I hung these up on the wall above our bed. The other three were the Emperor, Temperance, and the High Priestess. As I looked at them, I got a clear message as to what I should do with them.

One of the hardest things about being a Queen is that sometimes you will give commands that are very, very hard for your servant. Sometimes they have to be done even though they're hard, and oddly enough, that's easier for me to deal with. I have to do hard things in my life too, and so I just remind her of that, buck her up, and try to be a role model in doing the things that must get done. That's part of being an adult. It's harder when it's something that I really want or I really think needs to be done, but I could live without it if it was too much of a hardship for her. How do I know if it's too much of a hardship? I ask her, of course, and get her opinion, but sometimes she doesn't know herself. Sometimes she thinks that she can't do something but when I push her through it, she finds that she can. This is empowering to her. Sometimes I think she can do something even though she protests, and she tries anyway and fails, and that makes things worse. Those three cards spoke to me. The Emperor said: *Be in charge. Push hard. You gave that order for a reason. Make them do it, by force of will or bonds of honor or inspiration.* Temperance said: *Be merciful. This isn't the right time, or she needs more help before she can accomplish this. Back off and don't be stubborn.* The High Priestess said: *The initial task may not work the way you defined it, but you can come up with a compromise that will meet your needs and hers. Be creative and think outside the box.* When Pathia is protesting an order because she thinks that she can't do it, I take a deep breath and ask God to tell me what I should do, and I draw one of those three cards. God hasn't failed me yet. And I don't think He will.

On Becoming More...
Master Ron K

I have been with my wife Dixie for just over thirteen years. For the most part, we work together in a relationship of equals. I know this sounds funny coming from a long time Leatherman and Master, but that is how I see it as having evolved. I know that there are many that wonder over the equality of our relationship, but I no longer have those doubts. Do I often make the decisions and set the tone or direction in our relationship? Certainly. But I have come to see us as equal partners with an equal investment in the success or failure of our relationship. If either of us lets up on our efforts to build a better relationship we both fail, so we have equal responsibilities and obligations to the success of our relationship.

When we started out, we had what I would describe as a rather standard Master/slave relationship. Dixie was new to the leather world, and a slightly submissive but fairly heavy masochist. I was a rather experienced, very dominant personality and a heavy sadist who had been involved in leather and the Master/slave lifestyle for a number of years. After a short courtship, I simply claimed her as my slave and she agreed. Unfortunately, in those days I was just a tad (to be read as *way*) too internally centered, and not all that connected with the spiritual side of myself. Nor, if you had asked, would I have been at all willing to acknowledge that part of myself. As a result I really didn't manage my part of the relationship appropriately. After about a year Dixie wisely withdrew her consent to be my slave in an effort to protect herself from my damaging narcissistic behavior. I came very close to losing Dixie at that point, but for some reason I was blessed to not lose her completely. I believe that because we loved each other very much, we slowly developed our egalitarian relationship. After another year or so, we had recovered enough that we agreed to get married, and we have been married for eleven years at this point. I see this as just another point of evidence that we were clearly committed to our relationship, not our *roles* in the relationship.

During this long period of egalitarian exchange, I worked on my understanding of myself, the forces that drive my desires, how my spiritual needs are interwoven with each aspect of my life, and how we work with, live, and love each other along the way. As a result of this difficult and often painful work I found, looking at our relationship, that I had not honored Dixie's spirit well, and most certainly had not treated her spiritual needs with any real respect. It is difficult at times when I think about that period in our lives, because I remember just how badly I treated her and how badly I fooled myself into believing that I was right in the flawed decisions I was making that affected both of us so negatively. Today I continue to work diligently to build up my understanding of my spiritual beliefs. I work to implement them my interactions with Dixie and other people in my life. Put more simply, I try to be a better human than I once was.

These days Dixie and I are a committed couple. We have weathered some very troubling and trying times during our relationship as a result of that commitment. We still play hard when we have a chance and the time and energy to enjoy it, and we are working to build our mutual understanding of how our relationship works and how we affect each other's spiritual well-being by our actions. We have not formally resumed our Master/slave relationship—who knows; we may never get to that point. But we do discuss it and our mutual interests or disinterests in most things Master/slave. If asked, I'd have to say that the odds are that we will go in the direction that I want to explore as long as each of our spiritual needs are being met and protected. Sometimes we explore together, sometimes we have to walk our own path. So for us, the question has become: is it necessary to call it something besides a deeply loving and committed relationship? We are not so sure that it is.

I believe that in the Master/slave community our relationships most manifest themselves as spiritual in the way our behaviors interact to empower us as individuals. When I examine our rituals and practices—whether they are codified or just habitual—I can see how the energy flow affects each of us. Our underlying rituals and practices are generally designed to build the bonds between Master and slave. The words "spiritual" and "sacred" mean different things to each of us. Some of us put religious value and context to these words, but I do not. I look at these words as classifying the intent of our rituals to strengthen our relationships and our commitment to them. I believe that for most Masters and slaves, the relationship that they forge using ritual, mythology and metaphor are considered sacred to the parties in the relationship. In my opinion it is only by recognizing the ways that ritual, mythology, and metaphor allow us to communicate with our subconscious mind that we learn to use these tools to our advantage. We all have a basic set of practices taught to us as we were growing up. Subtle modifications to our already existing beliefs and practices can have huge impacts upon our relationships.

When I think about how things work for Dixie, and I can see the simple act of lying in bed snuggled together when we first wake up is so empowering and fulfilling to us. I feel so very connected after one of these deep snuggles. It feels like this ritual enhances my very soul. As we have begun to pay much closer attention to finding ways to be present and careful with each other I see that care often taking on ritualistic form. There is a comfort in the ritual and a reinforcement of our trust and love. Sometimes the rituals we are creating with each other have very explicit meanings that are discussed and planned. At other times the rituals just grow into something that is effective and necessary to our bond.

For me personally, the word "spiritual" speaks to the internal reserves of energy and light that I carry within me, and that I see in each person with whom I interact. It is used as metaphorical shorthand, allowing me to describe in one word a complete concept of human existence and the pathway to the subconscious mind. I see all forms of spiritual practice and ritual as the work of developing a conversation with our subconscious mind. Sometimes as a Master I will set tasks or rituals in place that are designed to help my slaves to strengthen themselves at a subconscious level.

I see the word "sacred" as something non-religious as well—it describes the way I view and treat the connections between beings, with each connection as a discrete and individual unit that deserves protection. For me it is not a necessity to be in a relationship with someone to feel some desire to protect that spiritual connection. The connection simply exists, and that is all I require.

I was raised to be a minister, well schooled in the world's various religious beliefs, yet those religious beliefs all failed to teach me very much about taking care of my spiritual self as a unique individual with individual views, needs, and experiences. The dogma of religion was just too inflexible and uncomfortable for my spirit. The dogma seemed to me to be completely focused on the worship of some supernatural spirit, while it ignored the spirit of the individual at so many levels. Further, the god I was taught about while growing up was not someone that I wanted to have a relationship with. He was always angry, jealous, and vengeful. I have never been an atheist or even an agnostic—I just didn't want to associate with a god like that. Anger, vengeance, and jealousy are not the kind of energy I wanted in my life, yet it seems that is exactly what I ended up with for so very long. As I have been able to develop my internal dialog and a relationship, I have found it much easier to let go of the hold that anger, vengeance, and jealousy that so infected my interactions for years.

I had been struggling for years to find a way to have my necessary internal spiritual conversations when I stumbled upon the work of Joseph Campbell. Reading his work freed me from a need to use any particular religious representation of god and the unknown spiritual world to gain access to it. What I am finding today is that I can use an amalgamation of many different techniques and representations to discuss or externalize what I am sensing of my own internal spiritual landscape. I do not need to subscribe to a particular religious view to communicate with someone about my spiritual path using the terminology and language that they use to represent their path. I simply need to understand the language of their path. I believe that there is something powerful in each of us, and the process of trying to understand and communicate with it composes my spiritual journey. My conversation with this part of me has enabled me to see how my actions can either empower or disempower me at the spiritual level. I can also see how the actions of those around me contribute or drain spiritual power, so I have found that I must be much more careful in my choice of associates and how I manage myself around them.

Because I am learning to attend to my spiritual path, I have begun to develop a relationship with a god of my understanding and the universe as a whole. I am able to see how the many things we do in life can contribute or detract from spiritual health. Most importantly, I think that I have begun to understand and see how fragile the spiritual connection with others is, and how it must be fostered carefully to allow it to grow and strengthen.

For the majority of my life, I was ignorant of my own spiritual underpinnings. I fought even the thought of anything spiritual as a part of my rejection of organized religion as a whole. Unfortunately, this allowed me to develop some very bad habits toward those that I was in relationships with, so my real struggle is discontinuing the battles and bad habits of the past, and forging new and more rewarding habits. As my spiritual understanding of myself continues to deepen, I recognize that I must be much more careful of my actions and decisions regarding those in my life, as I feel the impacts of those decisions in myself. I know that if I do something that saps or damages the spirit of someone that I am connected to, my spirit is also sapped or damaged. When I do something that improves my spiritual surroundings, I benefit and my spirit is enriched.

On the other hand, Dixie is an atheist, and I find that it is often very difficult for me to understand her point of view on spiritual matters because we do not share a common reference. While I know in my heart that we have a deep and abiding commitment to each other, the process of trying to understand her needs in this arena leave me thinking we are at cross purposes. Dixie's atheism often takes on elements that feel to me as if they are diametrically opposed to my purposes. Fortunately, because of our commitment, we are discussing this part of our lives together with careful understanding and communication, but the going is slow because of the differences in language that is being used—one spiritual, the other secular. This conversation is, however, progressing, and I find that in making the effort to understand her language and beliefs, I am more clearly able to understand and define my own. She tells me that it is helping her much in the same way.

For me, the difference between a "spiritual" and a "secular" power exchange relationship is nothing but the language used to discuss it. Each type of relationship dynamic has a language that is shaped by its very nature. But I have come to believe that they have a common set of goals and objectives. Some people are well-served using a secular approach to everything in their dynamic. Others are well-served in using a mythology or metaphor that is rich with spiritual language, and some, like Dixie and I, are learning to both develop our own shared language and pay much more careful attention to each others' original base language. Regardless of what mythology or metaphor people use, they are doing so because it best suits their style of thinking and interacting with others. The real challenge is how well each individual understands his spiritual foundation and the tools that it provides for strengthening the relationship as a whole. Are all of the parties to the relationship using the same system to communicate? If not, have they agreed on a translation between the systems that will work for them during the process of building the relationship?

Does Dixie consider me her "spiritual superior"? I would hope not. In fact, if she did, I would be shocked and put off. In my spiritual world view, each of us is a unique and individually empowered being with an independent world view and life. When we choose to engage in any relationship, we do so with the goal of building a new entity that contains the relationship. To be successful, the parties must be fully and equally engaged. The rules by which we agree choose to interact have nothing to do with better/worse, bigger/smaller, more/less powerful. They are simply the agreed-upon rules of interaction, with each party to the relationship having a specific set of responsibilities to the relationship. For this and many other reasons, I do not use the term "power exchange" for our relationship because it carries too many implications that I consider diminishing or negative. I simply use "authority exchange" to describe it, because regardless of what metaphorical system we choose, the end result is that one party agrees to grant the authority to someone else to make decisions for something in their lives, and at some level that they find spiritually satisfying. It is this accepting of someone else's judgment and decision making processes that allows them to find a more direct path to spiritual empowerment.

As a Master, I feel that accepting that grant of authority helps me to find a better place in myself and enhances my pursuit of a spiritual path. As my spiritual awareness deepens, so does the importance of my protecting and respecting this special gift. I also believe, as I reflect more deeply on the nature of this grant and its acceptance, that I would be unable to reach my full potential as a human without having it in my life at some level. In some respects, the challenge of accepting, protecting, and enhancing that gift is what helps me dig deeper into myself to find hidden depths in my abilities for empathy and compassion.

The attention that a Master gives to the spiritual health and invigoration of those in his care is of utmost importance in spiritually-based Mastery. When a master is interacting with a slave, it is easy to see how the work impacts the slave's mental and spiritual health. If the relationship is healthy, there is improvement in the slave's spiritual awareness and well-being. Their dedication to their slavery strengthens. Their ability to respond to their Master's desires and needs deepens and strengthens. I believe that a Master must also take the time and be dedicated in attending to his own spiritual health and growth. Both Master and slave must become deeply aware of their impact on each others' spiritual health and are dedicated to protecting and enhancing that bond.

When I am asked which approach is better, spiritual or secular Mastery, I believe that a false choice is being created. Neither is better than the other—each has its own language, mythology and/or metaphor. When observing many of the discussions on this subject, there is some implication that one is better than another. I believe that this is most patently not the case. However, for myself, I find that the more I learn about my current model of spiritual mastery, the more I understand how I was unable to use a completely secular model to accomplish what I wanted. For me, a spiritual model gives me access to the fine controls and communications that I need to have in a good relationship, regardless of authority structure that has been agreed upon.

As for a "higher power," I think that we each have our own understanding of a higher power. For some it is god, for others it is their conscience, and for others it is karma. Regardless of what we call it, there is something there and we have a constant contact with it. When we do wrong or damage someone, our higher power is what speaks to us and what drives the remorse we feel. When we make amends, it is this thing that lives in us that finally allows us to forgive ourselves. It exists in every system, we just call it different things. Ignoring it or rejecting it as I once did will lead to disaster.

How we respond to this power is what is most in our control and what seems to drive us in most of our lives. Some of us try to develop a strong working relationship, and others do everything they can to ignore it. The results of each are only evident to each individual internally when they choose to be truly honest with themselves. But I will say this: I have never met a Master that was a true leader and good for those in their service who did not have a well-developed relationship with this part of themselves.

And what about the submissive in all this? I have been around and around with myself about this question, and I suspect that I will never have a good answer to it because I am not submissive. However, I do have an opinion. I think that a slave's most important goal must be that they allow their external reality to match their internal understanding of themselves. If a person is truly committed to being a slave, that commitment will drive their external actions. We cannot fight our own nature and expect to find peace. When I see situations where the stated commitment and the externalization of that commitment do not match, I also see dissonance. That dissonance is clearly visible and filled with pain. An example of this can be as simple as the slave that knows they are only permitted to have one drink a day, and who decides to have two. That slave must then fight with himself or herself over telling Master about the disobedience. Later, in the discussion with their Master, they will admit that they knew that they were limited to one drink, and yet they cannot describe why they disobeyed. The shame and guilt that they feel in this event is great and was avoidable. Their problem was that they did not live up to their internal commitment.

I find this very sad and difficult to be around because the slaves in this situation don't trust themselves with their own spiritual, mental, or physical well-being. I believe they must take full responsibility for it themselves, as their well-being depends completely upon their actions. This is a responsibility that I do not want and am unwilling to allow someone to thrust upon me. My personal expectation of a slave is that they are mature enough and mentally well balanced enough to behave in a way that is completely consistent with their commitments. Further, I expect them to have enough responsibility and integrity to come to me to discuss any area that they feel they may have overcommitted on so that we can correct our expectations before there is a problem. By doing this, we are able to create a much more tranquil and spiritual coexistence.

At some point in the past, I wish someone had said to me, "If you are looking for a spiritually-based relationship, you must decide if you are willing to accept that there is an incredibly powerful bond built when one engages on this basis." When you develop a relationship to a level of an agreed-upon authority exchange, you are assuming an even greater responsibility for your actions, because you now are directly affecting someone else's life, regardless of whether you are Master or slave. When this relationship develops into its fullness, there is a deeply spiritual connection that makes the positive or negative impacts on one felt just as deeply by the other. In this kind of relationship, I believe that the Master serves the slave every bit as much as the slave serves the Master. It is only through that in-depth understanding of the interdependency being created that a Master can help the slave to develop the kinds of spiritual/emotional/physical underpinning that allows them to become a full partner in such a relationship.

When looking at potential partners, I try to gauge their understanding of their own spirituality and their dedication to developing a deeper understanding of it. It is the commitment to their own understanding of their spirituality that empowers them to become a full partner in an authority-exchange relationship. This understanding and commitment allows them to be truly clear with themselves (and me) about how they view and are able to process their chosen position.

The power and depth of the entwinement that can occur in a Master/slave relationship is an amazing thing to watch as it develops. I wish that when I'd started out, someone had been able to get me to see just how much damage I was capable of doing while I was still trying to sort out my own internal and spiritual confusion. So for me, the most important goal is my own internal spiritual clarity and an understanding of how connected things in the world really are. We affect each other in ways that are amazing and wondrous. We can channel that effect into positive developments if we can stay focused. When discussing Master/slave relationships, I tell people to get themselves very clear about the reality of their internal terrain. That is where the most danger lies, and for most of us those dangers are covered by years of practiced denial. Lack of clarity and focus can lead to abuse or worse.

Our relationships are all about becoming more than we are capable of being by ourselves. For us to be successful, we must strive diligently and unflinchingly to build our relationships on the solid bedrock of our shared truth. For me, the responsibility of being a Master and of interacting with slaves has helped me to discover parts of myself that I never imagined existed. I am *more* because of those in my life that have been or may be in my service. My spirit is full and joyous.

I Am Goddess ... she is worshipper

Ms. Simone and lisangl

Worship. Just the word itself lends to the divine, the unknown, the ethereal.

Worship elevates the item, focus, or person being worshipped to a new level of existence and opens the worshipper's soul to love, oneness with that focus, and enlightenment. This is the mainstay of all religions: worship. It can be anything from communing with Mama Gaia to Born Again Christianity. Whatever background one stems from, there is the element of worship. This concept even reaches into our lifestyle as fetishes, desires, and goals. Slaves desire to worship at the feet of their owners. Reverence for one's partner comes into play in many M/s relationships. How many of us have witnessed, on completion of an intense scene, the submissive kneeling at the feet of their mistress/master in sublimation?

When I began in the M/s lifestyle, the concept of the divine making its presence known within my power dynamic relationships was not even considered by me. Having the divine cross over into, and even become, the mainstay of my personal M/s relationships never dawned on me. As far as I knew, I was just having a good time throwing energy around, pulling and manipulating chakras, and giving incredible rushes to my play partners. That all changed when I met my property, lisangl.

Back in the late 1980s, spiritual BDSM was not as vocalized and acknowledged as it is nowadays. It was reserved for the arena of body modification. I wish there would have been a shaman, mentor, or spiritual Master to help guide my steps. As a practicing witch since age 15, I was aware of the trancelike state one can reach through mediation, chanting, and such. It did not dawn on me that similar could be reached with heavy play, extreme scenes, and energetic manipulation. When I began to discover this on my own, I was like a kid in a candy store. I over-saturated myself with energy play, causing negative side effects from taking in bad as well as good. Kind of like mixing types of alcohol, I felt drunk. With practice, I learned how to filter out the bad and take in the good, increase its strength and return it positively to my play partner. With my ownership of lisangl, part of her service was to help me increase my control of energy manipulation and grow spiritually into the true Goddess aspect within. At this part of our path, our focus is on teaching others about the spiritual power dynamics. By giving back, we continue to develop our own skills.

I am a hereditary witch, born into a female maternal bloodline of witches. My grandmother trained me in the practical knowledge of herbology and spell-casting. Women on both sides of my heritage are mediums and psychics. Raised Methodist, I attended Bible camp each summer to age 13. The other half of my summer was spent with Grandma. My Aunt is a geriatric nurse who works in nursing homes. Part of her job is to escort their spirits to the next level. Ancestral work is a big part of my spirituality. If asked to identify myself I would first politely decline, but if pushed, I would have to say I am a Celtic Earth Witch with energetic and psychic abilities.

Lisangl states: "The path to meeting and serving my Mistress seems to originate from completely opposite perspectives, and yet by divine connection we managed to arrive at the destined meeting place of our journey. I was raised in a church atmosphere steeped in tradition and conservative views, and yet come from a long bloodline of mediums and psychics (prophets). Many of the conversations and family stories I heard as a child, in addition to the visions I have seen, have come to pass. A majority of my work, in addition to serving my Mistress, involves escorting spirits to the next level, assisting others with their spiritual journey, and communing with my Native American ancestors, while devoted to the healing of the soul of man and Earth."

Though our beginnings were starkly different, Mother Gaia drew our paths together to allow lisangl to serve, as she needs, and me to develop as a spiritual player capable of fully owning another. Until my skills developed and I grew as a magician, I could not fully assist her in releasing the inner controls she maintained, preventing her from completely giving herself over to me.

Before lisangl, I had kept my two worlds completely separate. My focus when playing was on the power dynamic of pain. A magician's greatest skills come from the transformation of pain, either his/her own or someone else's. A very talented magician is such because they feel pain more so than others, and can channel it into power and energy. Within our lifestyle, this concept is often hinted at but until recently, never fully disclosed. Many of you are familiar with terminology such as subspace, top high, or altered state of being.

Pain is where lisangl and I started. It was familiar ground for us both, one we knew we could grow from. I manipulate energy through administering pain to my partner, allowing them to let go of this level of existence and access a higher one. Without my knowledge, my play had been moving towards the spiritual. Now with lisangl, I was and am becoming more aware of it. From the start, we both were able to play harder than we had with others. Pain flowed from her to me, transforming into energy to sustain me. Transformed, it then flowed back to her to widen her senses to the divine within her.

Lisangl's desire to worship me was an uncomfortable one for me. With my background as a professional domme, the word "worship" alone struck a negative chord within me. (When a male client states he wants to worship, it implies oral sex.) As we grew together as a Mistress/slave couple and discovered each other's spiritual nature, we discussed the concept of the Goddess within oneself, and as her servant, lisangl's desire to pay reverence. Sexual union plays an important part in our connection and allows our energies to co-mingle. Through servicing me, she pays homage to the Goddess.

Our journey together took a halt when lisangl began having mainstream life issues. Upon reviewing the facts, we both feel it was necessary. We had gone as far as we could with the pain, bondage, and more visceral type of play. It had enabled us to establish our physical connection to the highest point we could take it with our current skill levels as spiritualists. Now collared, Lisa needed time to grow into her own as a medium. I, on the other hand, met my soul mate and future husband. He became my teacher in channeling my energetic talents and helping me acknowledge my powers as medium.

After a two-year break, lisangl returned to me. At this point, our dynamic took on a deeper reverence for our connection. She had a lot of internal struggle while absent, and one of our goals was for her to give up ownership of her chakras. Now let me clarify here; I do not say *control*, just ownership. I needed to allow her to retain the ability to manipulate them if she need to for creativity, sex, and magic. However, they were to become completely open to me, with nothing hidden or held back this time. We play together within our chakras, opening them to each other. For without being spiritually open myself, how can I manipulate hers ethically? Learning how to help her experience *kundalini* helped me get a better handle on my own.

When I do ritual, I tell my mate and lisangl so they are not only aware of what I am doing but so they can be alert for the energetic shifts within themselves. Part of lisangl's service is to shield and protect me when performing ritual. As her owner, I provide her with energy when she needs it, and shield her from harmful energy. Most of our play now is linked to tantric work designed to open the *kundalini*. Power dynamic relationships are perfectly suited for the passive approach of opening one's *kundalini*. Within this approach, one surrenders to another more experienced at manipulating the energy. This is called *shaktipat*. By playing with chakras, opening them, and moving the energy towards her crown chakra, it helps remove inhibitions and impediments to her awakening. This is a temporary state, however. It allows the surrendering one to sense the *kundalini* awakening. One of the possible side effects of this awakening can be a perpetual state of orgasm. One of my desires was to reach this awareness with lisangl so that I had her orgasming non-stop.

Another aspect of our power dynamic is the heavy strip-down of lisangl's ego. For a long time when we started, she held back. I would ask her if she desired to experience some activity; she would tell me no, then later in her journal admit she desired such. My rule became total honesty. Only with this could we move to the higher levels we were meant to. Part of her training to do this required extreme humiliation play. The removal of her ego from our interaction enabled her to serve me without thought for herself, her desires, or her wants. She focused completely on pleasing her Goddess.

Through our spiritual power dynamic, both my slave and myself feel oneness with each other and the multiverse. Our spirituality has become the main stay of our relationship. We communicate daily on our state of being. Instead of a simple "How are you?" it's "How are your chakras? Any changes, desires, fears we need to explore?" "How is your energy level?" She tells me when she needs help crossing a spirit. I inform her when doing a heavy casting so she can add to my resolve. Our service has taken on a higher level in which we not only serve each other but through each other, our ancestors, spirits requiring our assistance, and others seeking to develop this power dynamic in their own M/s relationship.

She is my soul slave, the one I claim as mine for all eternity. Even when parted, there is an energetic leash connected. Through her, I have allowed myself to experience the true giving of oneself. When her last chakra opened unto my ownership, our connection shifted into one of complete trust and connection. She felt safe even without a safeword. I felt at peace with my power. Our power dynamic shifted from Mistress/slave to Owner/property. I own her down to her core. The power in accomplishing this can be very heady and difficult to control as you develop an appetite for it. She has helped me access my inner divine and allow it to breathe. For so long, I lived in denial of its existence, afraid of ridicule from others, even within our community; at the time I was not aware there were others such as myself out there. We found our spiritual tribe, connecting with other spiritual power dynamic players in the community.

I have found that while I enjoy playing with others on a base level, that it is only truly satisfying to me when there is an energy or spiritual exchange between myself and my partner. Without this power dynamic, it now feels empty and cold. My magician within reaches for that type of play and desires to connect with another on that level. I can see the pain radiating from others and empathically seek to channel and change it via BDSM play. Lisangl gives herself to my sadism, knowing it needs to be sated. By doing so, I learn to control the ability to administer pain and raise the awareness of those I am administering to the possibilities for a spiritual awakening via catharsis.

I am as she needs, she is as I desire.

Anarchic Christian Submission
by Elizabeth, a.k.a. Blessed_Harlot

My honey and I met for the first time online, in a LiveJournal community called "christianhippies". That was seven years ago. We now live together in a lifelong commitment. He is my Daddy, Sir, Mine, my leader, and my "Vr Srs Dominate", among many other things. I am his Cunt, his Slut, his Babygirl, his submissive, and His.

While we don't have a traditional 24/7 D/S relationship, I might be called on at any moment to submit to him, to follow him, to take his desire as my guide. It is both of our desires that I also be whole, wholly myself, and that my autonomy remain intact and nourished. I am a feminist. We reject binary gender roles, and are egalitarian in the structure of our relationship. Since we are both made in God's image, we make decisions together, shape our bond together, and explore together what power exchange looks like without the presence of coercion or spiritual violence. We even create our scenes together, through the interactive collaboration of his leading and my following. It is part of the sacred paradox of our relationship that I both share responsibility and submit, that we are egalitarian and D/S, and that I am his and my own, and God's first of all.

We are both Christians (though we do not resemble any D/S-practicing Christians we have met). The core values of our faith are also the core of our sexual ethics, and the basis of our D/S relationship. Three of those values are body positivity, anarchism, and power deconstruction.

Body Positivity—We Are Beauty

To introduce the concept of body positivity as it applies to our lives, I'd like to use my honey's words, from a love note he wrote to whoever would read it:

> You are beautiful. Yes, you. And no, I'm not saying that because of who you are on the inside. I'm saying that because the lines, curves, shapes, colors, textures that make you up are so uniquely you that your very

existence causes awe. You're not beautiful if you could just lose 5 (or 50) more pounds. You're not beautiful except for your scars or stretch-marks. It's not that you were beautiful when you were younger, but now you've got grey hair and droop here and there. You're not beautiful despite anything. You are beautiful because you are you and no one else can be. You are beautiful because your form has been exquisitely crafted by God/the Universe/your life to be precisely what it is at this moment. The process that you are, and the billion ways in which that process will present itself from birth to death, are beautiful. You are beautiful.

(Gabe, www.malakhgabriel.net)

We organize our spiritual life around the value that flesh is sacred. God made flesh and named it good. Jesus himself was a sign that God so loved flesh; God could not resist becoming flesh and experiencing such sensuality directly. Jesus gave himself over to becoming flesh, and he repeatedly valued flesh and fleshly needs and desires as worthy of our attention. The most basic ritual of Christianity—the drinking of wine and the consumption of bread in remembrance of Christ—unites bodily need for basic sustenance and spiritual need for intoxication with worship of the divine.

This love of flesh has many implications. To begin with, we are all beautiful—not when or if we meet an arbitrary cultural standard, but as a function of being ourselves. Bodies naturally have a variety of authentic gender expressions, and all of them are beautiful fleshly wisdom expressing itself. For flesh needs no striving or fixing to be worthy of love, but is merely and easily holy itself. Our needs for food and shelter are sacred, as is the striving to feed and shelter all of our human family. Our bodies' unique gifts—like my gifts for submission and Gabe's gifts for domination—are sacred, and worth exploring in healthy ways, because they are extensions of who we are, as this unique flesh.

I have always had in myself what I consider to be gifts for following. While they're not "textbook" submissive traits, they do create in me a natural tendency to mold myself to someone else's direction, when I choose to act on those tendencies. This world is not always a safe place to take on direction from just anyone, and growing up with such gifts and sensitivities has often been a difficult road. It has been a vital part of my health to learn when to refrain from following, when to assert or be firm or stand my ground.

Our D/S relationship is so very special because it is built on me having the safe space, the joy, and the release of indulging those gifts and following him—following his wishes, following his pushing me out to my growing edges, and following his lead in building scenes. It is in finally coming to an understanding of these gifts of submission as sacred (in a world that doesn't truly respect submission) that I feel I am giving appropriate respect to God's creation of me.

Any self-expression, by its very nature, is my own exploration of God expressing Godself through me. The ways our bodies connect and communicate through desire, arousal, intensity, and ecstasy have great value in and of themselves. My beloved and I pursue many things because they arouse our desire, and that in and of itself is something we value as a part of our relationships to God. The pleasure, pain, peak experiences, and mystical connections that our bodies are capable of are gifts we treasure. I don't consider myself a masochist, though I have learned how to "process" pain and put it to good use. It is the act of taking in intense sensations that my honey gives—through spanking, caning, and cropping, for example—that allows me to feel I am fully respecting my God-given gifts and capabilities. This means that each time we cherish our bodies, each time we revel in the sensations we can produce, each time we give ourselves over to pleasure—and pleasurable pain—we can do so with gratitude for the abundant, fleshly life God has given.

Anarchism as valuing consent

We are also both called by our faith into a commitment to anarchism. We experience human government as the ultimate shitty play partner; it relies on coercion and nonconsensual, non-negotiated violent acts for its very existence. We cannot opt out of government's control over every aspect of our lives. There is no negotiation, as there is no ability for us to say "No". We all submit to a multitude of laws and rules that shape our existence every day—including, among many others, business-driven rules of where we are allowed to congregate, and when; labyrinthine regulations on what we are allowed to do with our own property or how long we are allowed to keep it; a host of laws about what we are allowed to do with our own bodies, and where and when; and tight strictures on which individuals and how many of them we are allowed to be with in legally-recognized relationship. On top of the codified coercion of all, it has been made clear over and over again that our laws are not enforced equally among a diverse population. We also submit to the continuous rule of other, law-enforcing human beings that may or may not treat us with whatever measure of dignity the law allows, depending on how human they perceive us as being. Some live with the threat of violence from authorities simply because of who they are. If any of us do not submit to these laws or to the rule of the law-enforcing class of human beings, we potentially suffer various consequences that are, by their very non-negotiated nature, violent. Sometimes the violence extends to physical restraint and bodily harm.

My honey and I reject that such violence must undergird human community, and we work to create alternative spaces of intentionality and respect. Part of living out our faith is to be aware of how we use our power in community. Anarchism, for us, is about living out consent in community. We strive to speak openly about consent and to encourage intentionality around leadership and power exchange. Gabe is not a dominant person in general; he doesn't impose those gifts on anyone. His domination, like my submission, stems from consent within specific relationships. A D/S dynamic was not taken for granted either in our relationship or in his relationship with his other primary partner; in both cases, the dynamic is unique and carefully negotiated. All of our authentic relationships, with or without a D/S component, are built on a foundation of egalitarian power with one another. Consent is paramount to respecting the personhood of others.

While the BDSM world knows well how critical the issue of consent is, it lies at the heart of our personal values because of Christ's teachings first. Jesus repeatedly revealed issues of power and control, and he intimately connected consent and human dignity. Many of Christ's instructions, understood in their original context, were about power—about giving consent to how one will be treated, about standing up to coercion, about choosing one's submission very, very carefully.

For one telling example, look at the now-famous "turn the other cheek" passage. As we take in Jesus' instructions about a very specific situation, it is critical that we understand some of the cultural context Jesus' listeners would have lived every day of their lives. "If someone strikes you on the right cheek..." Jesus described (Matt 5:39). In Middle Eastern culture, then and now, the left hand was physically unclean and inappropriate to use to touch any others. It was the right hand that was always used to strike someone in public. To fight like a respected man in a brawl with a social equal, one threw a punch which would land on a man's left cheek. For someone to strike you on the right cheek, they were making a statement about your worth that resonates still today in Western culture. To strike you on the right cheek, they were backhanding you. Jesus' instructions to his working-class and poor followers, on the occasion of them being humiliated in public by a wealthier and more "respectable" citizen, was not to retaliate with violence. It was not to run away. It was *not* to simply cower and accept this treatment. Consider what defiance is involved to respond with a blow by turning one's face back to the assailant in a way that requires them to change their actions. Jesus tells his followers to stand their ground, turn the tables, and demand to be treated as an equal. To "turn the other cheek" (Matt 5:39) was to demand a fight that gave each man equal power and status. To turn the other cheek is to refuse to accept coercive and non-negotiated domination. (The author Walter Wink can tell you more about this idea.)

This is one glimpse of a larger strategy that Jesus instructs us in at every turn: to set our terms of engagement with others based on love, respect, and egalitarian uses of power. It is this boldness, this profound respect in Jesus' teachings that gives me the courage not only to require respect and equality in all of my relationships, but also to kneel before my beloved willingly, and receive his instruction.

Power Deconstruction and a theology of power exchange

Jesus continues his deconstruction of power dynamics throughout his public life. Jesus constantly questioned both religious and civic authorities, redefining righteousness, love, community, even Kingship. He described a King with little earthly power, who relied on the hearts of human beings to create His kingdom. When religious authorities made holiness about restriction, he made it about inclusion. When his friends were hungry on a day when religious rules forbid them to find food, he valued the needs of human bodies over authoritative rules for holiness. He explained, repeatedly, that even among enemies, there is no proper place for power-mongering, nor even disrespect.

Christ's radical restructuring of power is a lifelong task for an attentive Christian to understand. His teachings touch every aspect of a follower's life. For my honey and I, practicing power exchange illuminates Christ's teachings. We use the unique gift of erotic power exchange to unpack our own uses of power, our interactions with it, and our choices in confronting it in everyday life. By giving of myself in submission, I come to know consent and my own power like I never did before. I see Christ's teachings come alive in my life. Each time I give myself over to follow my beloved, and then purposefully leave that sub space again to return to daily life, I learn something new about my choice to do so. I learn something new about my power, and how I give it away or keep it, every day. I learn something new about how I submit, or don't submit, to God. Power exchange becomes a spiritual devotion. I see power exchange (consensual and nonconsensual) more clearly in my everyday life. I see how power dynamics unfold in my workplaces, in my friendships, in my communal life. I see them more clearly because of our intimate power practices, and then my faith gives me tools to preserve my integrity in the face of coercion.

Placing power exchange at the heart of both faith and ethical sexuality comes naturally to us. BDSM is often a foreign idea—or even anathema—in conversations of feminist sexual ethics. We are in solidarity and agreement with those who object to the systems of oppression we all live in: systems that enforce sexism, racism, classism, heterosexism, gender rigidity, and other violent degradations of human integrity. However, rather than believing BDSM to be the intimate reinforcement of such violence and coercion, we know it as a sacred space for deconstructing that violence, and breaking through into transformation of it. For us, BDSM, and D/S in particular, is uniquely suited to this work.

Embodying our Values

Body positivity, anarchism, and power deconstruction—these are a few of the threads we can tease out from the ecstatic, indulgent, purifying, edifying tapestry we get to weave from the gifts we've been given. On any given day, the snapshots of what this looks like change.

My honey and I have followed our faith by drinking consecrated wine from each other's flesh. We have strengthened our faith by exploring my instilled fears of rape and abuse, while wrapped in one another's arms in a safe setting. We pour on liquid wax, in faith; as my flesh is burned and then separated from the outside world by the liquid-solid mass, finally to be broken out and made free, we are reminded of the sacred resurrection of Christ, and the continuous resurrection of life and love in the world.

I have had the uniquely liberating experience of being beaten for wearing clothes, and for all the ways I cover my beauty and don't allow the world to see it. I am often wrapped in rope—carefully, lovingly, as a reminder of the bonds of slavery our God has liberated us from, and as a physical manifestation of the bonds of love between us. I wear a collar—his collar, as he is Sir. It echoes the bond I once had to church communities, wearing their collar to serve God in covenant with them. In serving my beloved, I am reminded how intertwined his flesh and my flesh is with That Sacredness we both serve. We explore our furthest boundaries—him seeing just how he wants to push me, and me seeing how far I can go—because our life of faith is about following our Lord in an exploration of sacred risk.

In constructing our spiritual life, we draw from established Christian theology and traditions, and from established feminist and nonviolence writers, as well as from our own personal insights. And we are grateful to stand on the shoulders of wise writers and call them mentors and guides. But we don't personally know anyone who integrates these things in the same direction we do, who follows this same path. The loneliness of that is difficult some days. The fruits of this journey, though, have been great, and my gratitude is profound at sharing our life just as it is with friends and loved ones. I am proud to submit to my honey. And I am thankful to follow a God that liberates, whose yoke is that of freedom.

You can read more about Elizabeth and her honey Gabe at www.pornocracy.org, a pornographic documentary of their lives together.

Holy Surrender

Of Slavery And Service

Lee Harrington

(Originally published in Sacred Kink: The Eightfold Paths of BDSM*)*

Being a Slave does not mean you have to be submissive in all of your life. Some of the strongest-willed and most self-sure people I know are Slaves. This is because there is awesome confidence to be found in knowing that we have a role in the universe, and that we are stepping into the fullness of that role, that calling, each and every day. Even if we don't do service each day by chopping wood or carrying buckets of water, we are doing the work of refining our spirit, learning new things, investing in that which is owned.

It is this day-to-day work, of finding ourselves, of handing ourselves over to another (be it a cause, a god, or a human worthy of all that we are) that enables us to find more layers of ourselves. It demands vulnerability. It deserves to have you come forward, naked and eyes wide-open. Though our bodies may crawl, we who hear the calling of Slavery in our hearts walk tall with our head upright and looking forward.

We come to a moment, in our Slavery, where we find ourselves raw, naked of spirit, exposed, unguarded, unprotected, defenseless. Through a thousand different journeys and tools, the moment comes. Two paths lay before us. One path is to run. Run back to comfort, security, and a road that everyone will understand and you can explain to your coworkers and family.

The other path is surrender. Surrender of the body, surrender of the mind, surrender of the spirit. We each make a choice. Neither choice is wrong. It is not more exalted, more profound, or better to be a Slave. You are not the highest and mightiest on the totem pole of submission. You do not become the best beloved and gain super powers.

It's a calling, or it's not. Or it's not right now.

But if we do make that choice, if we are called with all our beings to follow the road that says *surrender*, an alchemical process takes place. In the crucible of surrender, with our hearts exposed and held safe by the universe and our Master alike, we can find a new route to growth, awareness, power, and vitality. And the amazing thing is that, as slave Caroline once said in her own thoughts on the matter, "the power a Master has is only equivalent to the extent their Slave is willing to be vulnerable. If a Slave is unwilling to be surrendered, a Master has little to virtually no power to make them vulnerable." This becomes yet another gift we grant to the one willing to walk the path with us.

You may be the best Slave in the world, with the deepest calling, but without someone willing to journey with you, walking the path together will not be possible. That is not to say that a Slave who has no Master is not a Slave. If this is your path, your calling, it is not needed to have a Master to serve as long as service and surrender takes place. Then what are you surrendering to? Universal Will. A cause. The community. God. There are so many things worthy of vulnerability, service, and surrender. Some will treat you better than others. Some give more direct feedback than others. But the choices do exist.

What makes a good Master/Slave relationship is not that it is always perfect, but that when troubles come, everyone involved rises to the occasion. Each person supports or makes space for the other's journey from a place of excellence in their respective roles.

The calling of Slavery and Service requires faith. Requires power. Requires love.

Becoming authentic is the art of the soul made visible. Not plastered on billboards, screaming I AM OUT from floats in a parade. If such things make you smile, enjoy them, but embracing the authentic self means trusting our instincts and letting that which we are cut from, what our true being is, shine. It is removing the clutter, clearing away the debris, and knowing ourselves.

Slavery will only help you be authentic if you are called to it.

You can be called to this work by having the siren song sneak up out of nowhere with one partner, or one place to serve. You may carry the calling in your spiritual work. Perhaps you choose to express the call through feeding the masses or clothing the cold. But others of us are called to express this desire through serving another human, or a greater good through a specific human.

Because this is what I am called to do.

And sometimes, when we shine, by walking with our heads held high (even when we are crawling), we give permission for others to find their own path of erotic authenticity as well.

Surrender To The Universe

dawn

In the time before time, before I knew of healthy M/s relationships or M/s relationships in general, life was different. I did not walk on a healthy path. I had been abused as a kid and swore that I would never be under a man's control again. I did not trust men in general, and though I married straight out of high school, to a man that rescued me from my home of origin, I didn't trust him either, in the long run. My marriage was rough. I decided to take charge because of the lack of trust. As for my spiritual path, there wasn't one. God was a man. Why would I trust him?

After a while, this life was not fulfilling anymore. I found that I wanted to trust men. I wanted to trust someone enough to want to take care of me. I wanted a spiritual life. I knew there was so much more than what I had experienced so far. I needed more. What I did not know was that the Universe was listening to me. When it was time, she started putting the stepping stones in front me that I needed to take. I just needed to be brave enough to step on them and move forward.

The first thing she did was to put someone into my life that had started on a spiritual path that I liked. He had a serenity about him that I envied. We talked about spirituality. We talked about recovery. We talked about trust and compassion. We talked about everything except sex. We really got to know each other, deeply. I liked what he had, but also found out that by talking, I was finding my own spiritual path as well.

Then, we started sharing more secrets. I started telling him about what turned me on sexually. I hadn't shared this with anyone before, not completely. When I had mentioned it to my ex, he had thought I was on the weird side, so I learned not to bring it up again. But I shared these thoughts slowly with the new person in my life. He thought my ideas were hot and started sharing some of his own. They matched mine.

The Universe decided to give me a bigger push. Not only was I finding my spiritual path and my sexual identity as a submissive, but

I got the big whammy thrown at me. It was time to start my healing journey from my childhood abuse as well. All of this happened at the same time, and through the trust of a man—something I swore I would never do—freedom was found.

I truly believe that the Universe put my Master in front of me, and it was my choice to be brave enough to accept the gift. I stepped into his embrace and surrendered to his guidance. He became the voice of the Universe. I do not see him as a God, but I certainly see him as a vessel, as a voice of the Universe. Through my Master, direction is given. This has been shown to me time and time again. Because of this, I've learned to completely trust him and his guidance.

Through this trust, I continued to explore my spiritual nature. Though he and I walk side by side on our spiritual journey, each of us is flavored a little differently, and his story is not mine to tell. But as for me, I took the spiritual principles he learned through his addiction recovery process, and added some of his Buddhist concepts that he lived by, and added it to my Wiccan training and shamanistic beliefs and ritualistic living, and came up with a spiritual path that I'm happy with, one that works for me.

At the same time, we were building a M/s relationship. This is the style of relationship that works best for both of us, though we also realize it's a tool for our spiritual growth. For me to be a slave and a spiritual being, there were a couple of things that I had to learn. One of those was surrender. I needed to learn to surrender to the Universe as I learned to surrender to my Master. They both only have my best intentions at heart. More than likely, this is probably why I developed my spiritual path at the same time as I learned to embrace my slavehood. I knelt for my Master daily to show my willingness to serve him. I knelt in front of my altar daily to show my willingness to serve and listen to the will of the Universe.

A Master/slave relationship, like working with a spiritual path, involves looking deep within yourself to find what you believe in. I found that I could believe in another human. I found that I could believe in a spiritual path (after being let down by my childhood religion). Each of these paths work hand in hand for me.

The Master/slave relationship demands that I lower my walls and allow my Master in. Without this ability, I would have never found my spiritual path. My Master requires complete faith in our life together. My Master requires complete honesty and transparency. My Master requires integrity and growth. Funny, so does the Universe.

Sometimes it is very hard to explain why this Master/slave lifestyle that I live is so spiritual to me. But I cannot imagine living an M/s lifestyle without it being spiritual as well. My spiritual life is not stagnant and neither is my life with Master. They both require me to grow as a person and be a compassionate person that lives based on "right action", not taking things personally, and doing my best.

Finding The Slow Path

Joshua Tenpenny

(Originally published in Sacred Kink: The Eightfold Paths of BDSM*)*

I did SM for years before I was introduced to the concept of the spiritual Ordeal Path. Up until then, I just did fairly heavy recreational pain play. It wasn't a cathartic or emotional thing for me. It wasn't deeply transformative, or even particularly meaningful. I didn't have any abuse issues to work out, or phobias to face. I just liked rough sex. It was very simple.

Then I had a few experiences—entirely unrelated to SM—that gave me a much more spiritual perspective on life. At first, it didn't have any impact on my play, but one afternoon a kinky friend was demonstrating bloodletting (venipuncture) and he drew some blood from me. To my surprise, I suddenly felt uncomfortable with the whole situation. It no longer felt right for me to treat my body and blood so casually. I felt like this should be a sacred thing, or at least a deeply meaningful thing—but I was unsure about what the meaning should be. In any case, I couldn't just drop the syringe of blood into the "hazardous medical waste" bin and be done with it. Under the pretense of wanting some fresh air, I went out to the garden and with an awkward whispered prayer, I squirted the blood into the earth.

I was raised only nominally religious, and this was the very first time in my life it had ever occurred to me to modify my behavior (especially my sexual activity) for purely spiritual reasons. It wasn't that anyone had told me that certain activities were spiritually "wrong," but after coming to this spiritual perspective where all life is sacred, some things became too powerful to treat trivially.

Many people I knew, including my master, did SM as part of the spiritual Ordeal Path, and I asked them for help in exploring this. I tried a few things, with mixed results, and eventually ended up at a gathering where a group of people were doing hook pulls in a ritual setting. There was an opening prayer, there was drumming, there was focused intent. It seemed like the perfect setting to really connect with this aspect of spirituality, to figure out what it meant to me. While waiting my turn to have hooks pierced into my back, I began to slowly pace the room. Walking back and forth, listening to the drums, the image that came to mind was of walking a long and winding path down to the underworld. It wasn't one of the symbols the group had used in setting the ritual, but it was present for me. After the hooks were in, and tied to the wall, I began to pull against them while interacting with my master. It was an intense sensation, painful, but not excruciating. I don't get an endorphin rush easily, but this did it for me, and before long my head was swimming and everything seemed bright and amazing. It was ecstatic.

After a while, that rush faded, and I was just standing there feeling nothing in particular. It seemed like the experience ought to "go somewhere", that there ought to be something beyond that rush. I knew what it felt like to be in the presence of the divine, to touch the deeper mysteries. This wasn't it. I experimented with intensifying the sensation by pulling more strongly against the hooks. It just hurt, nothing else. More pulling only led to more pain. The ritual seemed to be winding down by that point, so eventually I gave up, and went to have the hooks removed.

Some of the other people there clearly had experienced a connection with the divine. I could see it reflected in their eyes. But I hadn't, and I didn't know why. I packed up my things and went to leave the ritual space, thinking to myself that for whatever reason, I hadn't tapped in to whatever that ritual could have connected me with. When I got to the door, I felt an overwhelming push backwards that had a faint glimmer of what I had come to associate with divine presence. I paused, and I immediately knew that the ritual had "worked". It had connected to whatever it is that turns the symbolic acts of a ritual into an experience more real than ordinary reality. And because it was "real", I needed to walk back up that winding path from the underworld that I had envisioned at the beginning of the ritual. Frustrated, but respecting the truth communicated by that push, I paced the room again. When I returned to the door, there was no further push, so I left.

That night, I prayed. I wept and I prayed. If the ritual had worked, why had there been nothing there for me? Eventually I came to the end of my crying, and calm settled over me. With my frustration and anger and jealousy cleared out of the way, I could see that there had been nothing there for me because that is not my path. I remembered a dear friend of mine, a very spiritual person and a heavy player in SM. For years he had been reaching further and further, trying to connect to something deeper through his masochism. The last time I had seen him, he had just done a very heavy scene that took him further into his experience of masochism than he had ever been ... and yet, he felt it didn't take him "there". Like me, he had some idea what "there" looked like. He had reached it through Buddhist meditation. He said that if this scene hadn't done it, he didn't think any scene would. So he took a break from SM entirely and spent six months in a monastery. That was his path.

My own spiritual path is one of service and submission. Submitting fully to God's will is at the heart of many spiritual traditions, and while the concept resonated deeply with me, in practice I had no idea what God's will was. I could make some reasonable assumptions on clear ethical issues, but most of life is lived in the grey areas where it is interpretation of a principle that dictates action, not the abstract principle. (Does "Thou shall not kill" permit self-defense? A just war? Wearing leather?) I dearly wished for clear and unambiguous religious teachings to guide me. I flirted with Catholicism—or perhaps it is more accurate to say that I had a passionate unrequited longing for Catholicism, and not just for the awe-inspiring power of their ritual, but for the strength and certainty of their traditions. Unfortunately, Catholicism has no love for a kinky transgendered queer sex-radical Pagan like me. Some people can reconcile that, but it didn't feel right to me to pick and choose among the teachings of a faith where so many of my fundamental life choices and values were considered to go against the will of God. I know myself too well for that. I'm a slippery little weasel. I knew that I would continue to pick and choose as it suited me, avoiding any discipline that would require too much of me, reinterpreting scripture to validate whatever I'd planned on doing anyway. That wasn't what I was looking for. I wanted a firm hand to guide me.

I looked into other religious traditions, but I found none that I could embrace wholeheartedly. I asked my master for guidance, but his Neo-Pagan religious community emphasizes finding your own way and being true to yourself, not following any one particular set of rules. I tried to find my own way, but I kept coming back around to a concept I learned from Christian monasticism. The first chapter of the *Rule of St. Benedict* criticizes monks who have never lived under the rule of an abbot: "They live ... without a shepherd, within sheepfolds of their own devising, not within the Lord's. Their law is self-gratifying: what appeals to them, that they call holy; what they dislike, they regard as sinful." That rang true for me. As I attempted over the years to build a spiritual discipline for myself, this passage echoed through my mind. Eventually I accepted that I could not meaningfully surrender my ego to a discipline that my ego had constructed. This was a sheepfold of my own devising.

Again, I talked to my master about this. He is a shaman and Pagan priest, but he had been taking a hands-off approach to my spirituality. He tends to think of spirituality as an individual matter between each person and their gods, and he felt that, in this one area of my life, he had no right to interfere. However, as I submitted to him fully in all other areas of my life, it seemed appropriate at that point in our relationship for him to gradually and carefully take control in this one last area. I formally asked him to order my spiritual life, and to tell me how I ought to be following my spiritual path.

For a long while, I had assumed that the struggle to understand God's will and form one's own conclusions about spiritual matters was an essential part of spiritual development. I believed that simply following someone else's rules was an immature expression of spirituality, and that a meaningful spiritual connection transcends the need for such rules. From an intellectual and political perspective, I would still prefer to believe this. However, for me, years of philosophical inquiry did not bring me one bit closer to God. It did not make me a better person. It did not aid me in making good choices with my life. It did not provide comfort in difficult times. For some people, it does all these things, but not for me. When faced with decisions of spiritual import, I continually became mired in doubt and confusion. *What is God's will in this situation? How am I to know? How can I trust I see that clearly, as confused as my mind can often be? Am I mistaking my own will, or my own fears, for the will of God? Is this obstacle a sign I am on the wrong path, or a test for me to overcome? How am I to be sure I am doing it right? How can I be anything but biased in this?* The intellectual approach just doesn't go anywhere for me. It is not my path.

Submitting wholly to my master's will is so much clearer. I know exactly what he wants of me, and if I'm doing it wrong, he'll tell me unambiguously. I can't wiggle out from under a rule that challenges me by cleverly reinterpreting the rule, because he'll sit me right down and ask me, "Is that *really* what you think I meant by that?" I can't just follow the letter of the law, or look for loopholes. There is absolutely nothing to hide behind. I can't fool myself into thinking that I am better at this than I really am. I can't fool myself into thinking I am worse at this than I really am. I know exactly where I stand.

My master directs me in all ways as to how I am to live my life, but doesn't micromanage. He sets up the goals and ideals and priorities, and I do my best to live my life according to that standard. If I need clarification or assistance, he provides it, but I am a responsible and competent adult who can manage all the normal challenges of daily life. And it is generally a very normal life, compared to what people might imagine. There is no bondage, or chastity, or punishment. He never goes out of his way to inflict any hardship on me—he says that life provides hardship enough. It is exceedingly rare that he directs me to do anything that some other reasonable person in my situation might not choose for themselves. It might not be what *I* would choose, but it is always a reasonable choice. There is no fear of him asking me to do something ridiculous or harmful. In fact, he makes much safer and healthier choices for me than I would be inclined to make for myself. He has my best interest at heart.

Spiritual enslavement has also given me a different perspective on my body. From what I've heard from people who walk the Ordeal Path, physical ordeals change one's relationship to the body and the flesh, usually in an empowering way. Instead of taking that way of winning back one's flesh through suffering and triumph, I have turned over my flesh to someone else, and I live that as a daily mindfulness. Everything about the way my body looks, how I dress it, how I care for it, what I feed it, how I do my daily yoga practice, what markings are placed on it, is a reminder that it does not belong to me. In a hook pull, one's flesh and pain can be an offering to the divine through temporary surrender, but then you get your body back afterwards. My flesh is a permanent offering, and that surrender is my daily ordinary prayer. Instead of a doorway of dramatic ecstasy, this is a long, slow road of patient discipline. Of all the roads that BDSM can give us to the top of the mountain, this is the longest and least glamorous.

The tasks set before me by my master are in part his own will, and in part his interpretation of the will of the Gods. The distinction is of utmost importance to him, but as the years pass, I find it becomes less of a relevant distinction from my perspective. If I believe that it is God's will that I serve and obey this man (which I do), then it all amounts to the same thing. I am extremely fortunate to be in service to someone who has a very clear connection to the Gods. It removes all other questions, leaving me with only the struggle to surrender and obey. And believe me, that is struggle enough for one lifetime.

Discovering My Path

seresse

I have been seeking a path to the Divine most of my life, with a number of false starts and bumpy passages. I never dreamed it would take the form of a power exchange dynamic. I fantasized about being a slave when young, and yearned for it as an adult, but didn't connect it with any spiritual path until fairly recently. I would like to share some of that story, as it has been very illuminating to me, and may perhaps shed some light on someone else's journey as well.

My current power dynamic is moving on the continuum from vanilla boyfriend/girlfriend to Master/slave (total power exchange). I would say we are probably mostly vanilla in appearance with private Dom/sub dynamics. I feel I have submitted and become His slave more than He has moved into being my Master, though it is our intention and direction to become fully Master/slave. He does not allow me a safe-word, which pleases me—but He also doesn't put me in any positions where I would need one.

The only "agreement" we have really negotiated was when I asked Him how He felt about safe-words, and His reply was, "I won't allow you to have one." Which quite pleased me, actually. Otherwise, we have talked about where we want this to go, and what it means for us. It is His intention to have a collaring ceremony and brand me. We also have a very simple and straightforward ownership document that essentially gives all power over all aspects of my person and my life to Him. There are no escape clauses or caveats. This will be signed at the collaring ceremony.

At this point, however, we are more vanilla in our day-to-day lives and the way decisions are made. He often asks me my preference and seeks my input in a vanilla way, though there are increasingly other times when it is clear that He is feeling very much the Master. He then simply tells me how it will be and what I am to do for Him—which usually turns out to be quite mundane and pleasant. That being said, there are some major "real life" decisions that have gone His way and not mine, much to my distress and anxiety. He has no qualms about manipulating and pressuring me to get me to agree, even though I really don't want to and feel very uncomfortable with it, so I do feel very much like I have given up a lot of autonomy and power in the direction my life goes.

We have known each other for a little over 7 years. We started out expecting our relationship to be vanilla, and really didn't know too much about any other way. I had tried unsuccessfully many years before to become a slave to someone, and had decided that was a bad road to go down, so I had no intentions of exploring it with this man when we met and fell in love.

About a year and a half into our relationship, we moved across the country with two kids, two cats, four horses, and a dog. It was quite an adventure and very much over my head. He took it upon himself to direct the show to a large extent—and I was happy to let Him! About a year ago, I asked Him when He first became aware that He wanted to dominate and own me—and He said it was during that move. That very much surprised me. He never said anything at the time, but looking back, He did begin to undermine my decision-making input, manipulating me and pressuring me to agree with what He wanted to do, even though I was very uncomfortable with His demands. He was confident that what He wanted was right for us, but lacked the authority to simply demand it. It consistently worked out well, so my trust began to build. It became easier for me to let go of being in control. So I would say this dynamic has been building for about five to six years, but only two years ago did we actually start talking about it, admitting it, exploring it, making it acknowledged and ethical.

My current spiritual practice started about fourteen years ago with a correspondence course written by a disciple of an Indian Guru. At first I just read the letters, opening my mind to the information, the different way of understanding. Gradually I began to meditate, concentrating on the Truth within myself and all around. It is hard to define the structure of it, or call it a "religion", though it appears to be based on the Hindu religion. It quotes all holy scriptures from the Bible to the *Bhagavad Gita*, seeking the Truth contained within all religions and spiritual practices—that is, that there is only One Being, one consciousness that is expressed within and as each of us. We are taught to see the One in everyone and everything, coming into harmony with what is, finding that deep place of peace and compassion that does not presume to judge, knowing that the One is playing and all is as it should be. The practice focuses on the power of thought to create our experiences, and also teaches that the ego and the mind are conditioned and predisposed to see things a certain way, which limits our experience of the Truth. We each are responsible for our own experience, whatever the outward appearance may be. The goal is to become free from the limitations of ego and mind—not to destroy them, but to become free from their influence, to be able to watch with amusement as they spin out the karmic play of our lives. We are encouraged to see every experience and relationship as an opportunity to see ourselves in a deeper way, to expand our understanding and free ourselves from our limiting concepts and judgments.

My Master/partner does not have an overt spiritual practice, though He seems to have an intuitive connection with the spiritual heart. Sometimes He quite surprises me with His insight and rightness about things. He is allowing Himself to be influenced by my practice, by what He sees and experiences by being around me. He has seen how it works in the physical, and deeply respects how it affects me and the way I handle and respond to things, the way I think, which is so different from most people. He is now reading the earlier letters, though I am not sure how much time and thought He actually gives them. I have noticed a softening and opening of His mind and heart during the seven years we have known each other.

For me, the dynamics of our relationship fit right into the spiritual teachings and practice. As I have been meditating and practicing for so long, I experience pretty much everything in my life as spiritual, so that includes the power exchange dynamic. I consider this dynamic actually very powerful for my practice, in that it sets up the very conditions that give me great opportunity to become free from the limitations of mind and ego. As His slave, I am focused on service to another, rather than on my own desires and urges. As He takes control of aspects of how my life is run, my ego is challenged, often reacting with fear, anger, and all kinds of justifications and arguments. This gives me a great opportunity to observe the ego and mind in action, choosing to surrender to the power of my Master rather than the power of my ego and mind. When I do so, the bliss and harmony I feel are profound. The same words the sages use to describe the state of Enlightenment would be appropriate to describe my experience of surrender to my Master and His power and control.

We do not have any formal rituals that we practice to express or reinforce the spiritual aspect of this relationship. It is mostly my own inner process and effort. It feels like such a natural part of my inner workings to submit and surrender that I no longer judge myself for wanting to be a slave, but instead accept that this is my path, so I make use of it.

I have come to understand that devotion is an inner state or experience, and it doesn't matter to God what you devote yourself to, since God is in everything. So I devote myself to my Master, and hence find the bliss and peace that comes from devotion to God. I accept that God, or Guru, or the One, manifests and directs me through my Master, as it can be no other way. No one gets someone else's karma, so whatever happens in my life is my own karma, what I most need to further myself on my spiritual path.

I have no experience of a non-spiritual power dynamic, so I am unable to say anything directly about what that might be like. For me, everything is a spiritual experience, or it feels empty and unfulfilling. I find that when I forget (and I do) to look for the divine in this power dynamic, it suddenly feels empty, frustrating, and very uncomfortable. I begin to question my sanity and doubt myself. I begin to crave more and more intense domination from my Master, which He doesn't usually engage in, much to my frustration. Then I blame Him for the empty feeling, and start to think it is His fault that this isn't working, and that He is an inadequate Master. But when I remember to come back into my own center, when I remember to seek the divine in Him and in the actual moment, accepting the actual experience with gratitude, suddenly it is all fulfilling again, and I feel He is a wonderful Master, just right for me.

The two of us do not have any rituals or practices that uphold the spiritual aspect of this dynamic. It is an inner, private practice on my part, but I do share my experiences and insights with Him when we talk. He shapes the form of our daily interactions to suit Himself and His needs, and also to accommodate my needs for guidance and structure, but the actual spiritual aspect is left to me. I cannot tell that He consciously experiences this as a spiritual practice, though He is certainly open to the idea and that it is such for me.

Sometimes I can see how my spiritual practice is a way to serve my Master. As I surrender in devotion and come into harmony and peace, the space around me is affected, and all those within that space.

I usually do not consider Master to be my spiritual "superior", understanding that to mean that He is more conscious and committed to a spiritual path, guiding me. I feel that I am "superior" to Him in this regard as I have been consciously and conscientiously practicing for many years, and He has not had a conscious spiritual practice since He was an altar boy in the Catholic Church in His youth. But in other ways I do experience Him to be superior to me. He often seems much less inhibited by fear and judgment than I am, indicating more freedom from the conditioned mind and ego. I feel confident in His ability to intuitively know the right thing for us to do, even though He seems consciously unaware how much the Divine guides Him. There have been many times when I felt afraid and not trusting of His decisions, His plans, His path forward. I doubted the wisdom and sense of what He was doing—but every time He has led us to a better, bigger place than I would have thought. He does not meditate or have any formal practice, but it seems that He is guided nonetheless, simply by trusting His own intuition and inner wisdom.

It appears that He is just a regular guy going along through life with no real sense of connection to anything divine, no formal seeking of guidance from God in any form—but appearances can be deceiving. He is indeed connected and guided. We seem to complement each other well, me with the conscious practice, the words to explain and clarify, the lightness that comes from meditation, and Him with His intuitive wisdom and knowledge, His deep confidence in His ability to know the right thing to do.

When there is conflict, when I do feel threatened by His apparent lack of discrimination or regard for moral principles, I will approach Him with my concerns. We talk, discuss, explore. Often, I walk away feeling frustrated and not significantly reassured. In the early days it was really very distressing to me. I would spend time searching my soul deeply for the right path. And always it came down to ego vs. love. All my moral issues turned out to be conditioned value judgments that imposed limits on my ability to experience myself and the world in a bigger way. I would find myself in the position of having to decide which was more important to me: holding on to my deeply held and conditioned sense of identity, or letting it go and falling into the abyss of Love with my Master. Once it becomes clear to me that that is the choice, it's a no-brainer for me. That isn't to say it's easy, by any means! And it doesn't seem to get easier. Once one level is released, there is a period of happiness and bliss, and then a deeper level of limitations gets exposed and I have to go through it all over again.

As near as I can tell, Master isn't terribly affected. These wrestling matches are private affairs for me to deal with, and He doesn't seem to understand the struggle very much—or if He does, He leaves it to me to sort myself out. However, it does seem to me that Master feels such a deep sense of freedom and unconditional love from my submission to Him. I notice that the more I surrender to Him, the more loving and kind and generous He becomes. I would say that the most important quality for spiritual mastery is the experience that being a Master is a most humble gift, a deep responsibility, and must be guided by compassion and confidence. I say confidence because it seems the power is given completely to the master, and then he must use it, apply it, in some way that is bigger than his small ego self. That takes confidence in his inner path, his inner vision. I observe my Master to feel that confidence and go forward in some amazing ways that seem bigger than Himself. He very much applies that power to expand and improve our lives, our future, both physically/financially and also emotionally with more love, trust, play, lightness. In contrast, I have been in relationships where the "master" was focused on his own gratification. He used the power to please himself and didn't seem to feel the higher responsibility, or have the confidence to take that power and allow it to expand and make better our world.

I think the most important qualities for spiritual service and submission are a commitment to transcending the small sense of self (the ego); devotion; and trust—not necessarily in that order, but in a dance that supports and nurtures the process. I have found that devotion is an inner feeling that brings the sense of the divine into my heart, into my everyday life, regardless of what I am devoted to. It was hard for me to find that feeling, to surrender to an intangible God, to ask into the void for guidance and direction, and listen into that void, wondering if I heard/felt the Path correctly. To devote myself to the service of a tangible Master, a human being who is in my life, loving me and guiding me and caring for me, is much easier. That feeling of devotion now has an object to call it forth. I am able to experience that feeling of devotion, that divinity, much more clearly and strongly.

It seems that for every level of deepening submission, I must face some aspect of my limiting ego and let it go. This takes a great deal of commitment on my part to suffer the loss of my built-up sense of who I am, what my ego tells me should be important and that I should not give up. There are innumerable cultural and family ideas about what is right and important, about which parts of a person are acceptable and which ones aren't. These messages get internalized and become our sense of who we are, become our ego identities. In order to become free from the ego, one must become detached from these ideas of who we are and find the big I, the self that does not change, that is unaffected by all this stuff. I find the act of submitting to my Master and allowing Him to direct me deeply challenges my ego identity. "Oh, I would never do that—I am just not that kind of person. And certainly wouldn't enjoy it!" That is, until Master pushes me to really look at where that statement comes from, and I find that it is only my ego making noise.

This is my hardest obstacle. It is an ongoing struggle to keep my awareness on the bigger picture. My ego does have temper tantrums, fears, reactions, grief at losing so much of what I thought I was, and it can become overwhelming. I tend to blame Master for "not doing it right" when I am having trouble. Invariably, though, what brings me out of it into the light again is my own shift of perspective, taking responsibility for my own inner surrender and devotion, taking the leap of faith.

Which leads to trust. Trusting that there is nothing in this life that I will experience that I shouldn't. Trusting that Master is guided by God for my most effective practice and journey, even if He is unaware of it. Trusting that His journey is just as guided and supported as mine within our dynamic. Trusting that even in the deepest throes of ego panic and temper tantrum, this is the right path. Having the commitment to see it through to the other side.

I do not see that I have entrusted my soul to my Master, as such. I understand the soul to be a part of God and therefore not separate, really, nor mine particularly to give or not give. I have entrusted my soul to God, and I see God in everything, everywhere, including my Master. I offer devotion to God through my Master, therefore entrusting my soul to God through Master. If I had to submit to Master without this understanding, I don't think I could do it without causing myself a great deal of pain and diminishment. I would say that as I come to understand the power dynamic more intimately and deeply, the more I see that it resonates and is reflected in the religious aspect of my practice. It is like fractals, or holograms—each aspect of the whole is found in the smaller parts.

I fit well into a guru/disciple archetype, simply because that is the appearance of the path for me. That said, I don't really see my Master as my Guru. I understand the Guru to be the up-lifting, awakening principle of the Universe, and not really any single person. I look for that coming through my Master, while at the same time seeing completely that He is simply a man, with all the limitations and blind spots and issues as the rest of us. When I am devoted and in love, I see the Guru shine forth from Him. When I am resisting and caught in my limited ego drama, then I see Him as a pain-in-the-neck obstacle who can't do it right. So again, it comes back to my own inner experience and practice.

I'm not sure exactly what my Master's obstacles are, but from my observation, he seems to struggle with the idea that being a Master means not being a friend, that being a Master is something separate from being Himself in some way—a role rather than an integral part. He struggles with the idea that He will be hurting me if He allows His natural inner Master to do what He does. So perhaps He struggles with trust in His own inner nature, what that is, and that it is good and right. I see Him finding that more and more within Himself, finding that balance and confidence. He doesn't seem to view our dynamic as a spiritual practice, as such, though He is gaining great insights and experiences from it.

I tend to hesitate to offer advice, finding that often what is true and effective for me is not for someone else. The advice I do feel comfortable offering anyone for anything is to trust your heart and let it guide you. If you are seeking a spiritual power dynamic, one option is to simply see it in the power dynamic you already have. Look for a partner you love, you respect, you want to serve. But first surrender to your own inner divine and trust it wholeheartedly.

I can't imagine my path to this point being different than it has been. Would I have listened and would it have made a difference if someone had told me something, offered advice or guidance? Then

I wouldn't be quite where I am today, and where I am today is a good place. All the experiences and hard lessons I went through to get here have given me the knowledge and insights I have today. I wouldn't want it any other way. That said, I have found it amazingly exciting, reassuring. and heart-expanding to learn that I am not the only freak who is into this! Wow! There are so many others to offer support and advice and shared experience! For many years I felt alone and believed the messages about this aspect of myself being something that needed to be moved away from, not trusted, not safe. So I suppose that what we need to keep in mind as we explore this unknown is that to God it isn't unknown, and it wouldn't be there unless it was a useful path to the Light. Again, trust yourself, your heart, and have no fear of what dredges up from your darkest recesses—and remember that there are people to help and support you on the way.

Being The Lady With The Mead Cup
Kiya

The ritual fire is burning in the other room, and the witnesses are gathering. I have done my preparatory cleansings and purifications, and sit on the stairs, hunched over some music that will help put me in the right frame of mind.

It is my master's rite of passage, his self-defined progression into full status as a man. I want more than anything to be his *leman*, his comfort, his refuge, the warm nurturing bundle who helps him carry his emotions and bury his stresses through the challenges of this initiation. I want to be his support, even his cheerleader. I want this, and it is forbidden to me.

But I am the Master of the Challenge.

He is my lover, my fiancé, a dear friend; we have talked religion, magic, spiritual development, and other similar subjects since well before we were partners. I know what he aspires to, and more, I know the places he is most prone to fail. I am a caretaker of weaknesses, among my many other functions, and in this time and place it is my duty to reveal those weaknesses and demand that he account for them, for each place that he falls short of what he says it is to be someone who is numbered as a responsible adult.

I must expose him to the judgment of the witnesses. I must be hard, and cold, and not allow affection to sway me from my duty. I must reveal his standards before the ritual, and demand that he measure himself against them.

I parse through slights, moments of neglect, failures in my mind, sorting them into categories, phrasing and rephrasing each challenge in my own preparation. I will go into the ritual, and when I speak, my voice will shake only a little.

There is a motif that crops up again and again in many mythologies: the relationship between king and kingdom. In many stories, if the health of the king falters, the crops can be expected to fail; certainly, if the strength of the king falters, his prowess will not be of help to protect the land and its people from invaders. There may be challenges to pass, rituals to perform, feats of daring and potency required to demonstrate oneself worthy to rule.

In some of these stories, rulership is an erotic partnership between lord and land. True kingship only exists with the assent of a particular woman. In some stories, she is the daughter of the last king, who has no son, who chooses her husband and the land's next ruler; in others, she may be a mysterious nymph who, with the proper respect paid, may provide the secret to overcoming the plague that has overcome the land. Or perhaps she is a hag who demands favors for her secrets. She is the personification of the kingdom, and she wishes to choose a hero to govern her, because if she picks a dud she will suffer from the deficiencies of the mystical pairing. When she is divine, she is called the sovereignty goddess.

The sovereignty goddess is not a passive, compliant woman. Indeed, she is often actively a warrior who must be subdued or pacified by a would-be monarch. She may be free with her affections, as a self-determined woman may choose to be, and she is also quite likely rich, beautiful, or fertile—for who would want to rule a land that was not any of these things? And how many fairy-tale bickerings between Prince Charmings over an imprisoned princess would be so much the more interesting if her authority as the goddess who embodies the rulership of that land were taken into consideration?

Obviously, this does not lend itself to clear and clean simple lines of power: this is the dominant partner, that the submissive. Instead, power becomes a complicated feedback loop, a meshwork of distinct, individual points; there is no kingship without a land to rule; a weak ruler degrades the land; a skilled ruler guides, supports, and encourages the land to flourish; a strong ruler is obeyed. The anthropomorphic personification (thank you, Terry Pratchett!) of the kingdom, that sovereignty goddess, must have standards for who she will accept as a governor. Once those standards are met, she will bow her head and be the transformational vessel for power, not only that which is gained by having her, but all that is poured into her to hold, protect, and convert into wealth. Ideally, the interaction is beneficial to both parties; that which is governed is not merely protected and utilised by its master but enhanced, developed, and guided to reveal still more of its potential, while the ruler gains not only the use of these resources and the pleasures of the property, but a taskmaster who will require the evolution, maintenance, and flourishing of the capacity to rule. Each improves the other.

Yet I am ruled, and he is my master. I am the manifestation of that which he governs, its goddess and its queen, and because he governs, I am his servant and slave. As I am obligated to pursue the fullest manifestations of the inner divinity that he calls me to become, he is obligated to be one worthy of harnessing that goddess to his will.

None of which illuminates what it actually means, in practice, to become a sovereignty goddess (or a sovereignty deity, if one prefers to use an non-gendered term), which is itself a path necessarily laced through with the concept of sacred power. It stands in direct opposition to the idea that a submissive partner gives up their power; after all, this is a question of divinity, and deities are not exactly known for being without immediate access to their oomph. The nature of my sovereignty goddess's power is not to rule, but to enact; not to decide once her lord is selected, but to enforce; not to govern, but to be a steward.

A lot of popular discussion of the power dynamics in BDSM operates through a conception of power that is heavily simplified, and often laced with pejorative approaches to lack of power. To be submissive is often framed as being lesser, as a position of degradation or lesser worth; even if the dominant partner is not conceived of as some kind of perfect and infallible entity, they are often at least portrayed as a superior being. This tends to lead to my own master muttering something to the effect of, "Just because people are doing different jobs doesn't mean one is better than the other." Obviously, operating within a system in which being submissive is conceived of as a humiliating experience was not one that worked for us.

Instead, we pursued a path of mystical dedication. Thus, if I am a divinity of what he rules, then I must know myself well enough that he can know what he owns. My resources, my skills, my capacities are all his to govern and assign, which means that not only must I be aware of them, I must be willing and able to put them into action. As I gain more knowledge and skill, that which he controls becomes wealthier, more worthwhile, a better claim; the borders of the land expand to encompass more of the world, and I have the potential to become a more powerful goddess. Only the *potential*, mind; it is very easy to let parts of myself lie fallow and unplanted when there are other, more interesting fields to cultivate. Here, the guidance of a ruler can help support and enrich his lands, deciding when some realms should rest and recover, and when to move on to the next planting in the psychological and spiritual crop rotation.

Not only must I refuse to truncate myself, but I must be able to take in the guidance and desire of my lord and, in some way, make it my own. I may not directly share a particular goal of his—for one thing, I have no personal interest in the grad school he is currently attending—but it is my responsibility to feed and nurture his strength so that he can more adequately pursue those goals. I must be a grounding force, a supportive home, a land that provides sufficient that its king can occupy himself with things other than the minutiae of governance and wringing value and support from his territory. The goddess must be stable, secure, and strong enough to support goals that are not her own.

All of this extends into realms beyond the practical. I have been a vessel for dreams caught on a wild and misty night, holding them until they could be brought into his demesne. I have been the crucible for prayerful magic—where some people cast a circle to contain the energies until they are released, I have used my body to hold, work, and transform that power. I have, most importantly, held the space for something larger than myself, attempting to give this sovereignty goddess space to live and act within the world, an embodied existence that can grant not just the material mundanities of the service relationship, but the drive and aspiration to governance, hospitality, and improvement that lies within the realm of the spiritual.

The entity invoked and channeled in this process of apotheosis is not foreign to me; she is myself. Most particularly, she is a form of myself who is unafraid of her own power and her capacity for affecting the world, one who is willing to reach for and achieve her potential, and who is capable of taking in a partner's dreams and work to bring them to fruition. The sovereignty goddess is self-willed and powerful, able to defend herself, bounteous, fertile, fierce, and wild; she sets her own terms for what she will accept in a partner, for she knows that a weak partner will reduce her strength.

In order to become her, I must discipline myself to self-knowledge and honesty: the boundaries of what I am must be known to me, and the resources that lie beneath the surface must be within my comprehension. I must give up hesitancy to stand up for myself, as I must be as resolute and fierce as any defense my master would make for what is his. I must not minimise myself, self-sabotage, engage in an excess of humility, or otherwise denigrate or reduce the territorial holding commanded by that divine power. I must strive to fully realise my own capacities, because only when I am fully and most completely myself am I most able to manifest and inherit the power of the sovereignty goddess.

At the same time, I must exercise care and diligence in the partnership I form. As legends such as that of the Fisher King indicate, when a sovereign is mystically partnered with the land, his health, stability, and prowess match the health, security, and bounty of the land; if he fails, then so does the territory. As the personification of that holy land, it is a sacred duty to select a king who is a match—and to encourage him to most fully realise his own potential as ruler because, as his strength and spiritual development grow, the goddess can come more fully into being.

I have to remain centered in my own understanding of my divinity. Even if that is a power rooted in service, it is essential that I flourish as my own self. The land may be tied to the king by mystical bond, but they are not identical, and if the land's needs are sacrificed in order to serve his aggrandizement, then eventually the roots of power will fail and the whole system will die. Thus, it is not enough to say "Have I fulfilled these orders and met these desires?" but I must also determine if I am bountiful, if I am producing all those things that I am suited to produce, if I am rich with my own existence. As an ancient chieftain looks over the herds and makes sure they are well-fed and on the increase, instead of slaughtering them all in order to keep having grand feasts, my partner is responsible for not destroying my own internal wealth and, when possible, helping me to expand it. Service does not remove from me the capacity to be a complete human being in possession of dreams, goals, and ideals; instead, I take on with my service the obligation to most fully pursue them.

There is a dual nature to this partnership. On the one hand, I am that which is governed, the land that falls under his sway. He determines many things about how things will be conducted in his territory, gives direction, and provides guidance, and I must strive to serve and fulfill that will. There is a sacred trust to be had there, now that I have elected to serve. The control and discipline is its own form of spiritual dedication, service to a lord rather than to a god—but again, he must be able to be the sort of lord who could be the consort and ruler of a goddess. He is as called to reveal his inner divinity as I, here.

On the other hand, I am the deity of that which is governed, and must be approached with appropriate reverence. The land does as it is told, to the best of its ability; its goddess tests the ruler to be sure that he is strong, and expects veneration, for there are few goddesses who tolerate being addressed with a lack of respect. Mine is the guardianship of the gates of wisdom, the initiatory road to greater power and rulership, and I am never permitted to put down that question, that challenge, that ascertainment that governance is in place. It is the responsibility of the king to provide hospitality to his guests, for certain, but without the graciousness of the goddess there would be nothing for him to offer.

In the holiest of times, in the most intensely focused moments, our shared discipline is one in which it seems the world collapses to nothing but the cycle of governance and manifestation, his will written upon and within me, my desire to bring it to fruition. There is that old rite of the *Hieros Gamos*, the ancient fertility ritual found in so many places: the seed within the land, the sex in the furrows of the field, to make all things grow. Within the sacredness of that presence, when I am most the goddess and he as much her consort as we may yet be, our union blesses all things that we strive to do together. His will is all, my desire is all; as we return to the larger world, that which is all pervades everything we do.

When we build these temples, we do so with care and deliberation. If I am to be the tablet on which he can write his desires, it helps a great deal for me to be clear ahead of time what he wants. I need to be in a place of trust and security sufficient, for a brief time, to be an entire universe to him, in which his every desire is enacted and supported as perfectly as can be done; we need to be healthy and stable with each other, as well as communicating with clarity and mutual support. It helps to not always have grand designs when building this pocket universe; building a space in which we can each have a pleasant erotic afternoon is as worthy a goal as any other, after all, and just as deserving of the attention of gods.

At the end of the ritual, my master presents gifts to all those who attended, who played a part in his passage to adulthood. Each is carefully chosen to reflect not only the person, but the role they played in bringing the process to a conclusion.

To me he presents two things. One, a wine decanter, a vessel that holds that transformational liquid for a time, the symbol of a gracious hostess or a diligent servant. One of the forms of the sovereignty goddess is, of course, the Lady with the Mead Cup, presenting sweet golden wealth to her lord and to his guests in a display of intoxicating beauty. Here is a classic image of submission and service, an echo of Ganymede the cupbearer, an implement for holding power and pouring it out as required.

The other is a knife.

The *Nature* Of M/s
"Gypsie" Ferris

Why stay together? We don't play, we no longer have a physical relationship, we don't even sleep in the same room anymore. His sexual orientation has changed and my M/s orientation has evolved. What keeps two people that have grown, developed and seemingly moved in complete opposite directions, together in an already difficult relationship, the Master/slave dynamic?

Everything changes, and relationships—whether founded on the M/s Dynamic or otherwise—change too. He was a heterosexual (and nearly homophobic) dominant male when I met him; and I was, I believed, one hundred percent submissive.

Experience and time slipped by. He became a Master, covered in his own right by his peers, and I became his slave. Through the security and trust formed within the M/s dynamic, both of us were able to branch out, experiment and experience new avenues of interest. Our commitment, formed originally within the parameters of a power exchange relationship, evolved and became more than the two of us could ever have predicted.

His interests eventually turned toward what had begun as a fetish and became his preferred flavor—young gay men, or "twinks" as that genre of gay men are sometimes called. I found someone else and made him my own for a time, discovering I truly enjoyed the top portion of the power exchange dynamic as well.

So how did we survive the turmoil, growing pains and real pain of such drastic changes? Love, commitment, security, safety, obligation, comfort would all be correct, but there is more. There is a deep affinity, a connection made between the two of us that became apparent from the very beginning. It is what has sustained us, nourished us, protected us even when we could not do it for each other. It is a tangible and yet intangible energy—a feeling of camaraderie, knowing, trust, and expectation. It is a belief in us as a unit, even when we are with others. It is a love so deep as to accept love from and for others.

The knowing of one another, this soul-deep knowledge and acceptance of each other, is our spiritual power. It comes not from physical intimacy, nor from material objects. It comes from an energy formed and forged over a period of time between two people, drawn together by Nature and the power of our own inner spirit. Nature and all that she holds within her womb is the spirit and power that cradles us, teaches us and supports us. For us, our spirit is renewed and refreshed by her everyday gifts, and we find our center in her and our rebirth. We find joy together in watching a hummingbird flit outside the kitchen window. It is this moment when we know we are connected by a power stronger and larger than we are, than any human is or can ever be. It is this then that sustains us, this indefinable energy provided by Nature and the Universe. Nature is for us, our Sacred Power and within her, we find calm when it cannot be found elsewhere.

That we came together through Nature, formed our spiritual interconnection, and created this over-lapping fabric of spirituality with and within each other, is in itself, evidence of a Sacred Power for us. He, having been raised within a Fundamentalist Christian background, dismissed all thoughts of spirituality and sacredness when he chose to leave that part of his life behind him. For myself, I was raised in the belief that there was one God, one Savior, and one Devil, but spirituality was never brought into the mix. One chose either good or evil and whichever way one chose, there you would spend eternity after death. But as we began to explore the Master/slave dynamic more fully, we found a sense of knowing—a sense of the world around us, a sense of self as we delved deeper into our own psyches and that of each other's. It was in this release that Nature made herself abundantly clear for us.

It began with a breath, that deep breath one takes after a hard flogging or caning and in the knowing that you not only survived it but relished it. In that moment when he leaned forward to touch his mark, the energy moved from his hand into me and mine back into his. We both felt it, both stilled as it happened. It was energy,

Nature's energy that had finally been released from the oppressive trappings of cultural and societal constraints and it was sweet and natural and powerful. This then, was surrender. Not to one another but to Nature and to a higher Power. This then, was the release found when ego was no more, civility was gone, and our own, true animal spirits had been released back into Nature's fold. This was the moment the relationship changed from the physical to the spiritual. It was the moment our souls recognized each other and the energy within us. This was what we had been searching for and what had eluded us for so many years, yet it had been right here inside of us since birth.

To experience that release together, that primal flow of energy, we evolved toward what we might be: knitting the fabric of our energy tightly together, forming one unit, one spirit within two different beings. With the tight canvas of spirit and energy binding us together, the physical manifestations of the earth and all that happens here are endured when need be and relished whenever possible. It is a calmness that sets into the center of one's body, or soul, as some believe it to be. It's when the energy within not only recognizes but joins with the energy without, and the two rejoice in what for us is our spiritual power—Nature and all that she is, made up of energy, light, power, compassion, and love.

That is what keeps this couple together against all the odds, against all outside considerations and well-intentioned advice. Our Higher Power spoke to us through energy and light, brought us together through the power of Nature and we, as mere human beings, do not want to destroy that for the sake of physical intimacy, financial comfort, or community approval. One's own Sacred Power is the most sacred of all, regardless of what name has been attached to it—Christianity, Hinduism, Judaism, Wicca, etc. It is what is produced within, the Sacred Spirit of self through growth, compassion and a combination of soul energy, sol's energy and that intangible yet tangible energy that is the living spirit within us.

Our belief in each other, in our power exchange dynamic and in each other as human beings, is strong. He will always and ever be a

Master and more, he will always and ever be my Master in heart and spirit, and I his slave. That is the way of it, and the way we want it to continue. What happens next is anyone's guess, but we are more than ready for the rest of the ride and journey; whichever way it takes us, whomever it brings our way or to whomever the path may lead. The strength it took to forge our original Master/slave dynamic, and the work and commitment it continues to take to keep it healthy, viable, and flexible allows us to enjoy the journey as Nature and the Universe desire. The M/s foundation—strong, solid, and formed on a dynamic as old as Nature—carries us through the turmoil, the heartache, the joys and achievements. Nature, the Sacred Spirit we have found together, takes that foundation and lifts it beyond the physical into a realm of beauty, love, commitment, expectation, and eternal hope.

M/s Relationships As Vehicles For Salvation

slave Rick

(Author's note: I realize this may be a controversial title. I also understand that the word "salvation" can be very emotionally charged, especially for those with a traditional religious upbringing. However, my hope is that you have a different understanding of the word "salvation" after reading this essay. In addition, for ease of reading, Master Skip has allowed me to depart from the Protocol of using upper case pronouns for Master and lower case for slave.)

I always considered myself a spiritual seeker. I was a seeker in the sense that I believed something outside of me had to be sought and found. It was spiritual seeking because I had faith that finding "it", whatever "it" might be, could lead to happiness and salvation from my pain. There's that word "salvation" again.

Regardless of whether you identify as a spiritual seeker, it seems to me that we all have an inner sacred longing. It is meant to guide and direct our lives toward ultimate fulfillment, if we don't get lost in the material and physical world along the way. It is kind of like our fetishes, in that we are meant to fully enjoy them without losing sight of the higher purpose to which they ultimately point us.

Most of us see with only our human eyes until our spiritual eye opens. On the material plane, this fosters the belief that more money, more sex, more power, higher position, the right house, the right job, the right relationship, and so on may bring the fulfillment that will satisfy this sacred longing. I decided, fairly early on, that the only thing worth seeking was a romantic lover/soul mate. If I could experience the depth of intimacy and love I craved, that would be the "it" that would bring me fulfillment. At least, that is what I thought at the time. It also seemed like finding the soul mate would mean I was validated, loveable, whole and just plain OK—something I clearly didn't feel most of the time, despite the outer disguise of my superior and often "entitled" façade. It took a while for me to discern that my "uppity" mask was about protection and a fear of being vulnerable. I certainly didn't want anyone to discover how ugly and inadequate I felt inside, no matter how successful the outer appearance of my life may have looked.

I also confused sex with intimacy at that stage of my life. If sex was good and greater intimacy didn't develop, I felt rejected and devastated. My hungry, needy grasping was very close to the surface and often tended to repel rather than attract others, and as a result, I felt unattractive. When someone rejected me or closed their heart to me, it tempted me to close my heart to them. I now realize that the real source of my pain was not the rejection, but the closing of my heart. I have since learned to better keep my heart open in the midst of pain.

In June 1999, I met my Master. He was co-facilitating a weekend called "Path of the Obedient Heart." I was brand new to the BDSM world, but something I had heard about slavery and "slave heart" touched a core place at the center of my being. That's what prompted me to attend this weekend workshop.

While Master Skip was an attractive man, he looked nothing like the men to whom I was usually drawn. I liked men to be bigger than me, stockier than me, with hairy chests and a very palpable "Daddy" energy. Master Skip was my height, weighed less, had a smooth chest and a youthful look that in no way conjured up a Daddy image for me. Similarly, I was certainly not his physical ideal either. Still, I was drawn by his confidence and his self-assurance. I could sense the power of his integrity. I marveled at the intensely focused, caring energy he directed toward those in service to him that weekend, and I longed to feel that energy directed toward me.

As the weekend concluded, there was a battle going on inside of me. While my heart shouted, "He is the one", my mind didn't quite get it. He didn't fit my mental picture of what I sought, yet I had never before felt such an intense "heart-pull" toward someone. That was my first spiritual lesson related to M/s: I discovered that my heart was more trustworthy than my head. I came to understand that what may be for my "greatest good" frequently doesn't match the picture I hold in my mind. If I remain too rigidly attached to my mental image of how it "should" be or how it "should" look, I miss what is in front of me that is absolutely perfect.

Luckily, I didn't miss it. I didn't understand it, but I didn't miss it. As the weekend concluded, I went up to Master Skip expecting to be my usual glib, articulate, well-thought-out self, asking him for exactly what I needed. I prided myself, back then, on being able to ask for whatever I needed. To my surprise, I had no words. I simply burst into tears. It caught His attention and we made plans to meet for dinner.

As it turned out, our dinner was the evening before my departure to spend three days with my mother in Florida. They were the last three days of her life. Up until that time, my relationship with my mom was the most intense one I had ever experienced. I intuitively knew there was a sacred contract between us—i.e. an agreement made by Souls prior to incarnating (according to the teachings of Carolyn Myss). In retrospect, I can see how completing that sacred contract was necessary in order to begin the sacred contract I have with my Master. As a psychotherapist, I see this sort of sacred contract in many M/s and D/s relationships. Whether the lessons to be learned are brief or for a lifetime, there is clearly a reason for the pair coming together, related to growth and Soul evolution. At least that is how I see it.

Master Skip was very clear that he was only interested in M/s relationships. At the time, I didn't fully understand or appreciate what that even meant, yet my heart said he was the one. So I figured I could play along with this "M/s thing" until he came to realize that I was his perfect lover and soul mate. Talk about egoic arrogance! I now know he is my soul mate, it just means something very different than I had previously understood. That is the wonderful thing about a spiritually-based M/s relationship. There is continual growth, deeper realization, greater awareness of self and other, until a point is reached where the "illusion" of self and other disappears into unity and Oneness. But I am getting ahead of myself.

Master Skip is a pretty intense sadist. I am not a masochist and have little or no ability to eroticize pain. Yet some of our SM sessions were incredible opportunities for growth. Many were about facing my fears. These SM practices became sacraments, administered at the hand of my Master through his Priest archetype. These experiences allowed me many sacred rites of passage. But more than anything else, SM gave me a glimpse into the workings of my own mind.

To paraphrase *A Course in Miracles*, the purpose of life is to learn how to change my thinking in any situation in order to be happy. A miracle is defined as a shift in my perception. I came to see that looking at an experience one way felt like hell, while looking at it a different way felt like heaven, and I had the ability to choose how I would perceive any situation.

I remember the first time I was single-tailed. I was terrified. Even the mere sound of the whip caused me to contract in fear. I tuned into my thoughts. It began with a thought something like "My body can't possibly handle this." If I followed that thought, the next thought might be "I am going to be torn to shreds!" If I followed that thought I started to weave an entire scary drama prior to receiving the first strike of the whip. I was hysterical even before being hit! This was that hell place I previously mentioned. In my general life, I realized how frequently I scared myself with mental stories of what might happen in the future. So much for living in the present moment! Gratefully, that lesson was eventually learned.

I began to understand that I could shift my perception about whatever was taking place. This was a major realization. I recognized that I could stop the running of a scary story in my mind by not following the rising of my first thought. Instead of engaging in a mental story, I allowed my body to relax, open and surrender to the whip. I allowed myself to feel my Master's energy move into and through me via the whip. Thoughts are terribly seductive, but you don't have to identify with them. Instead, you identify with the Consciousness that is aware of the thoughts. As I kept my mind one-pointed and still, by not identifying with or following any thought into a story, I began to experience great Peace, deafening Silence, vast Spaciousness ... Heaven!

It was very similar to experiences during great meditations. Who could have known that connection and bliss were possible by fully accepting and receiving the sting of a single-tail whip! This prompted me to pay more attention to the workings of my mind in all aspects of my life, and in my M/s relationship in particular. In giving authority to Master Skip to have control over me, in choosing to be obedient to him, I realized that he could do whatever he wanted with me. Of course, I trusted he would only do that which was for my highest good, since I do not condone abuse masquerading as M/s.

While I find trust to be a pre-requisite for obedience, I am keenly aware that trust deepens with time and experience together. I have come to realize, after almost 12 years in an M/s relationship, that there is no bottom to the depths of trust, and with each new depth of trust comes a new depth of surrender, and a greater alignment of will between slave and Master. There is something quite awe-inspiring about this recognition.

In many ways, my relationship with my Master became a metaphor for life. Although I worked very hard to create the "illusion" of having control in my life, in reality I saw how little control I actually had over what happened. It was similar to life with my Master. I never knew what his next order might be or what feeling his order might stir inside me. Yet if I trusted that the Universe, like my Master, was truly benevolent and wanted only that which was for my greatest good, perhaps I could let go and be less fearful of whatever life brought my way. I could trust that I had the full capacity to meet whatever appeared in life with gratitude, knowing that even the challenges brought great wisdom and lessons when met with surrender and acceptance. I could trust that the Universe was in full support of my growth and awakening out of the trance of egoic fear and suffering.

It's funny how you no sooner have a deep realization than the Universe immediately tests you. I was tested big time. A number of years ago, Master Skip experienced the loss of his biological family, resulting in significant grief. This made it very difficult for him to be present, even when we were physically together. I missed him. I missed the Master that I had come to know over so many years.

In fantasy, the Master is all-powerful, in control of every situation and always on top of things, particularly when it comes to the slave. But life happens, and the reality is that Masters are human and can find themselves distracted, despondent, and even depressed when facing such major life challenges as serious illness, the death of a loved one, or the loss of a job. During these times it may be all but impossible for the Master to provide the level of dominance and control to which the slave is accustomed. As a result, the slave may find it equally difficult to refrain from complaining, and to not feel resentful when they perceive that their needs are going unmet.

I recognized in myself this familiar, old pull toward resentment. In prior relationships, if my needs were unmet, it was time to leave. However, I had grown beyond this old "cut and run" syndrome. I knew I could choose to change my mind and change my thinking about the situation before me. I could perceive it differently, thus allowing a miracle to occur (as defined in *A Course in Miracles*). Again, if the Universe is in total support of my growth and awakening, then even this difficult challenge had some gifts to offer if I kept my heart open and remained receptive, accepting, and surrendered.

The first lesson was to refrain from taking what was happening personally. Master Skip was experiencing the grief that naturally followed a loss. I had done nothing wrong. I had not fallen short as slave. This had nothing to do with me. Taking it personally is making whatever happens "all about me"—a sure sign the ego is working overtime. That's what the ego is, the "story of me", and it is our mistaken identification with the "story of me" that perpetuates the lie that we are separate and apart from everyone and everything.

Next, I had to be transparent about what I was feeling. I was feeling the loss of his presence, so I was also grieving. You know, just like we have a digestive system for food, we also have an emotional digestive system. If we don't allow ourselves to process whatever emotions we are feeling, we can't digest and eliminate them. I had to share my grief with Master Skip, but with a clear intention not to change him, blame him, or make him wrong for what he was going through. That was the tricky part. I told him the innocent truth, with no agenda other than to let him know what was happening inside of me. I couldn't pretend that nothing was wrong because that would have been dishonest, and he has an uncanny ability to "smell" dishonesty.

Fortunately, Master Skip had already learned the lesson of not taking it personally. He was able to hear my loss and grief without using it to judge himself or to beat himself up for what he was experiencing. This transparent communication allowed me to see how his lessened ability to be fully present was actually triggering some of my old fears. As I perceived Master Skip's control with me diminishing, I felt the pull of my old need to be hyper-vigilant and in greater control in order to allay my fear and create the "illusion" of safety. It's funny how many things come back to fear!

Once I saw my fear clearly, I knew I had to walk my talk. I had to remember to trust the benevolence of the Universe, and to allow myself to rest in the safety of this realization. I had reached a point in my spiritual maturity where I knew that I drew all life experiences to myself in order to keep rubbing away any remaining rough, fearful, egoic edges. This was another rough edge getting rubbed smooth. As challenging as the experience felt, I could now see it as a test to determine whether I would betray myself and fall back into old fear-based patterns, or remain vigilant and surrender more deeply in trust and obedience to the Universe and to him.

I chose the latter. This allowed me to recognize that Master Skip still had control, albeit not the detailed level of control to which I had grown accustomed over our years together, and which kept me feeling safe. Still, if this lessened level of detailed control felt satisfactory to him, I could trust that it was also enough for me. This enabled me to feel my fear without falling back into old patterns of trying to take control.

Master Skip also told me that his Hermit archetype was very strong and he needed more alone time for healing. Again, I was able to refrain from taking this personally or hear it as my Master wanting less time with me. This wasn't about me. Instead, I heard it as his newest order. I heard it as my Master ordering me to serve him by looking after myself for awhile and giving him the "worry-free" alone time to heal himself. That sort of "reframing" made a huge difference in deepening my obedience in support of our M/s dynamic through this time of great challenge.

I also purposely allowed myself to recall, with great gratitude, my history with Master Skip. He had been there with his detailed attention and control during the many years I needed this from him. Now it was my turn to give the gift I had been given and to serve him in a new way. I don't mean that I was repaying a debt, or attempting to level the power playing field. It wasn't about getting brownie points that could later be cashed in by pointing out all that his slave had done for him or how indispensable I was to him. This was a very real opportunity to feel the joy of freely giving a gift with no expectation of repayment, no strings attached, purely out of love and devotion. I can sometimes be selfish. But here, I was being taught the lesson of simply loving without worrying how much I was being loved back or how much I was getting back. I understood, perhaps for the first time, that if I truly let Love be in control, *I* didn't need to be. When I gave myself fully to Love, I didn't always know how I would be used, but I intuitively knew this life would be used in service to Love, rather than in service to "the story of me". Another major realization!

I have mentioned fear and I've mentioned love. Let me come back to the word "salvation" used in the title. *A Course in Miracles* views salvation as the healing of the mind by dismantling the thought system of the world, which is rooted in fear, and returning to our "right" mind, which is rooted in Love. Usually, most of us are clearly insane and out of our mind (out of our "right" mind, that is). This "right" mind is the experience of returning "home" to Love. It is the direction toward which the earlier-mentioned sacred longing is ultimately guiding us. It is the same "home" toward which our fetishes can guide us.

Let's pull this all together to understand how an M/s relationship can be a vehicle for salvation. The *Course* says that the only thing from which we need to be saved are our own fearful thoughts. Our M/s relationship has helped me to dismantle many of the fear-based thoughts from my childhood, from the media, from our culture, and from our world in general. Such fear-based thinking has led to great suffering in my life. I don't think I am alone here. But as I learned to give the fear-based thoughts little or no attention by not following or identifying with the first thought, there was a sense of returning "home" to my "right" mind. This "right" mind is vastly different from the chaotic ego-mind that is in constant motion; always moving toward what it desires to grasp, away from what it fears, or against what it resists. It became crystal-clear that the needy ego-mind led to suffering, while the "right" mind led to a peace that passes all human understanding. The choice and best use of my free will was obvious. So it is in this way that our M/s relationship became a vehicle for my salvation. It "saved" me from the suffering caused by my own fearful thoughts.

When all mental movement finally stops and the mind is still, there is an opening of the spiritual eye and a deeper seeing. I now see that "soul mate" has nothing to do with having a lover or romance. It has everything to do with Love, but not the sentimentalism and barter deals that usually pass for love in our culture.

When the mind is still, it allows both the Master and slave to venture beyond the illusory boundaries of identity and ego in order to discover that Love is not a feeling or an emotion, but the very essence of one's True Nature. That is the Love I have come to know through a spiritually based M/s relationship. That is what I have learned from my beloved soul mate Master. And, through Grace, I can now see the same Beloved hidden behind every physical form.

That, for me, is real Salvation.

Salvation is the awareness, in the deepest possible way, that you and I are truly the same Love disguised as a person.

slave Rick is a kink aware psychotherapist working within the BDSM community in Los Angeles, CA. He can be reached through his website: www.KinkTherapistLosAngeles.com

Dancing With Life
Fiametta

I. Dancing With Life

He loomed over me, pounded into me. I challenged him force for force, clutching, clawing, demanding, and impaling myself further with the strength of my thighs. I matched the cruel joy in his eyes with my own glittering ferocity: I was Gaia, the Mother of Life, demanding pain and ecstasy in equal measure to feed my endless fertility. He pinched and twisted my nipples and bit my neck, still driving into me, I screamed out my climax and floated above delicious fields dark and rich. Luxuriously, I stretched, opening myself to the sky, seducing the rain into penetrating me, tempting the energetic sun into warming my flesh and my seed-children clamoring to be born.

I started breathing again.

II. Broken Beginnings

Growing up in an abusive family was an isolating experience. Bruises and burns had to be concealed, so my sisters and I were not allowed to play at other children's houses. All must appear perfect, so neighbor children were not allowed to play at our house. Mother could shift from raging virago to sweet-as-pie with the ring of a telephone. My father was in the military, so that every time we developed friends or found adults that might be trustworthy, we were transferred.

I had only myself to depend on.

I was very young when I developed a Warrior spirit. He/she was both summoned and frustrated by the tightrope walk of trying to protect my younger sisters from abuse, while not courting the same abuse for myself. At the same time, I always feared the power of anger: my mother was physically abusive to my sisters only when she was angry. On one occasion my own anger got away with me. When I was 14 or 15, I was so enraged with one of my sisters that I took after her with a knife. (Fortunately for both of us, she ran faster.)

In my birth family, the only emotion that was acceptable was anger. There were no words of love, approval was only given for excellent grades and clean rooms, and physical touch was nearly absent. I only remember my mother hugging me once. My father used to roughhouse with us, but that stopped when we reached puberty (only girls in our family.)

I stole a peek at our medical records once when I was in middle school, and was surprised to find out that all three of us had suffered from 'failure to thrive' in infancy. My mother used to brag about the 'efficiency' of her system of teaching us to hold our own bottles at an early age; and both my parents used to talk about one sister, who would be up on her hands and knees for hours, rocking, rocking, rocking in her crib, until it moved halfway across the room. They stopped telling that 'cute' story after the heartbreaking news stories came out in the 1990's about neglected infants in Romanian orphanages.

Neither of my parents showed any sign of spirituality while I was growing up. We were dropped off at the Protestant Sunday School on the military base once a week, and my parents drove off to have coffee and read the newspaper. At the cost of a quarter to put in the offering plate, it was the cheapest baby-sitting service in town.

To a spiritually and emotionally starving child, Sunday school was a foretaste of Heaven. Kind adults took the time to talk to me and listen to me. They told me stories, they hugged me. There were no hidden traps; they were not looking for ways to turn my own words against me. Eager to please these affectionate people, I listened to the stories, sang the songs, and absorbed the concept of a loving God somewhere out there.

As I grew older, I began to realize that all was not perfect in the white-bread Sunday school world. Some teachers were strict, some had prejudices, and most people spoke about a loving God, but behaved as if life was a deadly dull routine. Hymns with joyful tunes and soaring poetry were sung as though they conveyed leaden dismay. Fascinating stories from the Bible were meticulously dissected, dried, and laid out in formal rows, with all the juice and life sucked from them.

In the barrenness of my 11th year, I took a bottle of aspirin, emptied it onto my desk and counted out the number that I thought it might take to kill me. I contemplated them for a long time while I went over my options. Life in my parents' home was nearly unbearable, and life without love was unthinkable. But I was a smart kid and a stubborn survivor: suicide was too final, and running away would just ensure that I would be hungry and homeless. I unconsciously called on my Warrior for the courage to stick it out at home for the next four or five years, but I also decided that if life without love was impossible, that I *would* believe in a loving Creator. I said so aloud, alone in my room. I didn't care if it was the Christian-style God, or called by some other name—someone loved me.

III. Touch Me, Please

I always knew in my teenage years that when I let a boy touch me, it wasn't about sex for me; I was a "prostitute". I wasn't being paid in money; I was being paid in human contact—touch. It wasn't that I didn't feel any sexual attraction, but that was never my primary goal. Fast-forward to college and several boyfriends; some liked to touch, some didn't. I fell in love with the one who liked to touch—the one who was from a "touchy" family. Of course, that wasn't the only reason I fell in love—he was smart and funny and he thought I was gorgeous and smart and funny.

We married very young—I was 19 and he was 20—and while I knew I enjoyed exhibitionist, spanking, and bondage fantasies, I did not realize at that age that BDSM was fundamental to my sexual identity. We had a wonderful relationship: we were best friends, never ran out of things to talk about, and enjoyed a reasonably good vanilla sex life at the beginning. But he could never see the point of even the mildest BDSM, and some of it (flogging, piercing, etc.) was deeply disturbing to him. I loved him very much, I admired him for his magnificent personal courage, and I had to respect his views, as they were congruent with his personal dedication to peace, equality, and justice.

Very gradually, I began to lose interest in sex. I thought it was just the natural consequence of aging, or long-term marriage, or the difference between men and women. By the time he died (after 31 years of marriage) he had been ill for years, and my libido was completely shut down. But in some weird sort of self-defense, I didn't want anyone *else* to touch me: I was very uncomfortable with hugging, couldn't tolerate a massage, and wouldn't set foot in a beauty parlor or day spa or any place where a stranger might touch me. I was very, very safe behind those self-imposed walls, and lonelier than I realized.

After helping my husband through months of cancer treatments, and nursing him at home for months on hospice, I had nothing left. I sank into the swamp of depression. Everyone said how brave I was, how strong I was. I couldn't cry, my emotions were locked up. Except for work, I rarely left my house. If I dropped something on the floor, it was too hard to pick it up again—it simply stayed there. I felt like I was trying to move through ever-thickening molasses. The day that I sat at my dining room table, thirsty, for more than half an hour, because I couldn't remember *how* to get a drink of water—I realized that I was seriously ill.

Long story short, I got on the right medication (for me) and slowly began to engage with the rest of the world again. I decided to seek people who matched my sexual interests. I joined APEX and jumped in with both feet, naked, volunteering as a demo sub for a *Fire and Ice* class with Master Dennis, head of the Dragon Clan. (Well, it was the middle of the summer--who wouldn't volunteer for some ice play?) The woman who wouldn't get her nails done because it was threateningly intimate was letting a complete stranger impale her with a large ice dildo in front of 30 other strangers...

IV. Slave? Huh?

When I was first introduced to the man who would later be my master, and he suggested the idea of M/s to me, I rejected it out of hand. Four hundred years' worth of Yankee ancestors would rise up from their graves and haunt their unworthy descendant, I said. I invoked images of foxes gnawing off their own paws to escape traps. Obvious and visceral terror. I recalled my shock when a woman I knew years before had married a Saudi and moved to his country. How was any man worth trading freedom for slavery?

And yet! I had been reading John Norman's *Gor* books for years with fascination, despite the really dreadful, turgid writing style. The idea of female pleasure slaves devoted entirely to satisfying men appealed to me. I had seen similar ideas in other books and had developed them further in my fantasy life. But it all remained strictly fantasy—no way was I ever going to be able to trust anyone enough to let them put collar and chains on me...

But my Master wanted a slave, and I wanted him. I was tired of being lonely, and I wanted to give the BDSM lifestyle a chance. I watched, I learned, we discussed, we negotiated and renegotiated. I was very clear that being in domestic service did absolutely nothing for me. He did the laundry. I was just as clear that the idea of being a bedroom slave, a sex slave, was what turned me on. He used me twice a day, three times a day, whenever he pleased. He wanted a companion, someone to go to dinner with, someone attractive to show off. I modified my wardrobe and started leaving off the panties.

He taught me to love the floggers and the single-tail. I begged him to use knives, and he found that he enjoyed them also. I famously proclaimed that "I was not a slave," but I lived in complete surrender to my Master. Despite my ambiguous feelings, there were times when I was merely sitting at his feet and it felt like the most natural thing in the world. I was wholly engaged in love, gratitude, and peace; my own will surrendered, I simply existed in bliss.

We had many discussions about Mastery and slavery. He preferred the term "surrender" to the term submission, because submission meant giving in to a greater force, whereas surrender was voluntary. I agreed with him, and I also made a sharp distinction between obedience and surrender. Obedience is external: Master commands (wishes, desires,) and slave obeys. The slave might obey cheerfully or willingly or grudgingly or he might roll his eyes, but he does as he is told. Surrender is internal and cannot be commanded, only given. The Master can give the command, but there's no guarantee that what she gets in return is anything but physical obedience. Only as the slave begins to know the Master, and himself, and learns to trust that his Master can truly provide what he needs, can he increasingly surrender aspects of himself: body, actions, emotions, heart, will, and sometimes soul.

For me, physical surrender took only one encounter because my Master's deep concern for safety reassured me. But other sorts of surrender took longer as we began to know one another more deeply. How much did I want this type of relationship? An M/s dynamic was not on my radar before I met him, and I had only the sketchiest ideas what it was about. Gradually, I began to see how deep his need was for that dynamic, and I began to resonate with his need. I surrendered my actions, heart, and emotions one by one, and found great peace.

Surrendering my will was the hardest. I had learned how to set aside my will during my 31-year marriage with my loving (though vanilla) husband; to take joy in his joy, even though we might be doing something that I did not like. Contrary to all the jangling emotional alarms, I had discovered that giving up my own way once in a while would not kill me. But a M/s relationship was *all the time*!

After several heart-to-heart discussions, I became certain that my Master would not require me to do anything contrary to my ethical standards, and that if what he requested was problematical, he would be fine with amending or rescinding his command. I also knew his essential kindness; when he wasn't beating me, he liked to see me smile! That enabled me to surrender my will to his. I don't know how to explain the utter peace and feeling of belonging that were part of that deep surrender. When my Master and I were together, I felt a deeper intimacy in some ways than I had had with my late husband of many years. I learned to find peace in the ritual and dance of service, but part of me persists in regarding it as a game that shouldn't be taken too seriously, lest it be mistaken for something more substantive than it is.

V. M/S And My Spirituality

For many centuries, Western Christianity has been denying the sacredness of the human body. Accidentally or deliberately, the Church hierarchy set up a war between the realm of the body: food, sex, giving birth, and all the messy details of day-to-day life; versus the life of the soul: worship, prayer, God. In its fear of the power of the nature religions which preceded and sometimes cohabited with it, the Church has often rejected the sacredness of the natural world altogether.

The duality that the Catholic Church initiated in the 500-600's CE was even more emphasized and perfected by the Protestant reaction to Catholic bureaucratic corruption. Where the Catholic Church had once supplied images and gold-leaf to ravish the sense of sight, the Protestants gave plain white walls and a simple cross to concentrate the mind. The Roman Catholic Church appealed to the soul through the emotions and the senses, but taught its children to fear their bodies. The Protestant churches appealed to the emotions through the intellect, but they taught their children to fear death and fear God. The further we got from the author of Christianity, Jesus, the further we got from our bodies.

The work of BDSM is often centered on reacquainting spirit and body with each other. The pain of the single-tail or the thudding rhythm of the flogger override our left-brain emphasis on rational linear thought, so we can hear what our right brains and our bodies are communicating.

The M/s relationship I had with my Master, and the profound surrender I was able to access within that relationship, enabled me to reach out to my soul and to God/the Divine on a much deeper level than I ever had before. With my body at his command, I was paradoxically freed to go into my soul. With no responsibility but to remain surrendered and to obey, my soul and spirit soared together.

At the core level of my being, my body, mind, soul, and spirit were able to begin a work of integration worthy of any mythical epic.

On fortunate moments when I was paying attention, I was overwhelmed by the ocean of my soul's Divine energy, filling and spilling in ecstasies of light and joy, more immense than I could contain or even comprehend.

VI. Parting

For various reasons, my Master and I came to a parting of the ways. At about the same time that was happening, I went through an interrogation scene, a Rite of Passage, administered by Master Dennis, head of the Dragon Clan, and a helper. I needed to test myself—to know how I reacted emotionally/spiritually to being pushed over the edge.

They blindfolded me, tortured and taunted me with whips, floggers, electricity, pinches, pokes, blows, slaps ... I went down once, crying, and they let me be. I stopped crying after a minute and stood up tall again, determined to finish.

The scene proved to me that I need no longer fear my own anger—I was angry, but it was a "clean" anger. I didn't want to kill the men, or even hurt them; I just wanted them to stop hurting me! I could trust my own anger, and I could trust my Warrior. After the Rite of Passage, I began to feel even more integrated, whole and powerful, with sufficient courage for all practical purposes.

Although I do not enjoy emotional pain (physical pain is a matter of negotiation,) if the price I pay for loving someone, opening my heart to him, is the pain of loss when he leaves, I can embrace it. Every person is part of the Divine: sacred, beautiful, worthy of all love and all pain. I do not wish to love less, or less completely, but I do not think that I will be able to surrender to another person as deeply as I did to my Master, for a long time.

VII. Who Have I Become?

I do not need to trade my body for financial comfort or emotional security. I no longer fear that a touch, a rub, a tickle, or a hug will awaken the hungry animal within me. She's already awake. I and my body are friends, or even co-conspirators.

I can play in the dungeon or have sex because I want to and it's fun--but I never lose sight of the fact that every person I meet is infinitely precious and amazing. Sex should be wild and crazy and sweet and painful and hilarious and spiritual and messy and raunchy and healing and spontaneous and ritualized and sacred and earthy and hostile and nurturing ... and free. I am free to play simply because I love a person's laugh and passion and energy.

I believe that the spiritual path for each person is unique—in fact, *it* must be different, because we are each different inside and out. I realized at one point that utter honesty (with myself and the Divine) and transparency in all relationships was necessary before I could sense/hear/see/partake of the Creator/Love. I see myself becoming like one of those tiny sea creatures that are transparent: when you shine a light on them, you can watch their delicate heartbeats, see their food move through them; they have nothing to hide. Only transparency separates them from the amniotic embrace of the ocean.

Change, even painful change, has always meant growth and glory for me. So now, I am delightedly in love with and enslaved by only my Creator. My God, my Love desires me as I desire Love; Love longs for me, reaches out for me, caresses me, speaks to me, enfolds me in his/her warm, strong arms, flogs me when I need pain, pinches me to make sure I'm paying attention, penetrates me as I sob in ecstasy, and cries out for me to penetrate her/him.

Most of the time I am filled with so much joy that it's hard to contain, and our mutual bliss spills over onto everyone around me. The overflow lights the flame of joy in other people and they radiate it right back. It's a glorious feedback loop!

VIII. Goddess Dance

The Southwest Leather Conference was almost over for another year: another exhausting, exhilarating, exasperating weekend with friends and friends-to-be; crammed with information overload, testosterone overload, and the best drum section in the known world.

The final event was the Dance of Souls: a 3-4 hour ecstatic piercing, hook-pull, bell- and/or ball-dance. The hypnotic rhythms of tympani, bongos, cymbals, and indigenous instruments combined with the heated pheromones of nearly 200 dancers swaying, spinning, pulling against each other with ropes attached to hooks embedded in their bleeding and exultant flesh. The space filled with shouting, wordless chanting, bells, rattles, maracas, didgeridoos...

I found a wide, clear space close to the drums where the pulsing beat could rattle my cells right down to the DNA. Emotions bubbled up to the surface, demanding an exit with the same intensity lava demands an exit from the volcano. The invitation had arrived. I began a primal, primitive, ecstatic dance that was soon no longer under my conscious control. Left brain wisely stepped aside to allow right brain room to move.

I invited my emotions and spirit out to play, and they wanted to play with Kali: Destroyer Goddess, Devouring Mother, in love with anger and death. She and I danced as one, growling and snarling, channeling the stone-strength of Earth, the animal joy of rending and tearing She shares with Jaguar and Leopard, savoring the pain of the bells as We jerked and jangled them in my flesh.

Kali, sadistic Divine Bitch that she is, dropped me.

Hard.

I'm still joy.

Walking Together

The Path Of Devotion:
Gurubhakti In A Master/Slave Context

Raven Kaldera and Joshua Tenpenny

Raven:

Joshua had been studying yoga for a few years—and, as a sideline, Indian religion—when he came to me with the concept. He had by no means decided to be a Hindu; we are both staunch polytheistic Neo-Pagans. However, he felt that the concept of *gurubhakti* was something that came very close to describing the direction that our master/slave relationship was going in, and he wanted my opinion on it. After I had read about it and researched it, I had a shock of recognition: even as the word "guru" made me blink, I had to admit that this was described some of our practices on our path of spiritual service and mastery.

Joshua:

I wanted to explore *gurubhakti* because I really do adore my master in a way that is both personal and transpersonal, and I wanted to worship him in a way that was not self-serving for either of us. It seemed like a natural progression on our path.

I was told that one of the most fundamental misconceptions Western people have about Tantric sexuality is that they think it is about making your sexual practices more spiritual, when it is really about making your spiritual practices more sexual. Incorporating *gurubhakti* in your M/s relationship is the same way. What we're talking about is one way to position your M/s relationship in your spiritual practice, not how to create a spiritual practice that is based on your M/s relationship. If you have no meaningful concept of spirituality to build on, then this probably isn't going to be very relevant to you. Also, this is only one of the many spiritual roles an M/s couple might find relevant and meaningful to them.

Part I: From Darkness Into Light

Raven:

I was immediately uncomfortable when I heard the word "guru". That probably came as a side effect of being an American who was raised hearing that word as a negative thing, implying a cult leader who was egotistically charming his followers into shaving their heads, leaving behind their lives, allowing him to take sexual advantage of them in the name of "enlightenment", and turning over their money so that he could buy limousines while they begged in airports. I'd certainly seen enough media coverage of the ones who'd done just that, too. Apparently many Indian gurus just weren't prepared emotionally for the kind of temptation that would face them in America's capitalist and sexually freer society, and they succumbed to it, often in news-making ways. At its most positive, I thought that "guru" meant *someone who knows everything already, who is so much further ahead on their path than most people, who has rid themselves of most of the flaws endemic to being human.* This certainly wasn't me either. I've got plenty of flaws, and I know that they show. I've got a long, long way to walk down that road.

But the more I read on the matter, the more I realized that the word originally just meant *teacher*, in a formal committed way, vaguely like the Japanese term *sensei*. It didn't even have to someone who knew everything—just someone who had powerful knowledge in one area of life and living, and was willing to share it with others. The word is said by some Sanskrit sources to come from the Sanskrit words *gu* and *ru*, darkness and dispersal of the darkness—as some texts put it, leading from darkness into light. That image hit home as a major part of the spiritual mastery-and-service path that we have crafted together.

> *The syllable gu means shadows,*
> *The syllable ru, he who disperses them,*
> *Because of the power to disperse darkness*

the guru is thus named.
     –Advayataraka Upanishad 14–18, verse 5

As an adjective, the word has the connotations of "heavy" and "weighty", heavy with knowledge and spiritual weight. For us, this path is not play. It is work, it is serious, it is real, not a scene or an affectation. The above etymological explanation may also be, according to some linguists, an after-the-fact folk meaning, where the word was broken apart to poetically create the words for "darkness" and "light". According to them, *Guru* may actually be derived from either one of two Sanskrit terms: *gri*, meaning "to praise", or *gur*, meaning "to raise up" or "to make a great effort". In Tibetan Buddhism, the concept of the guru is present— probably inherited from India—and they are either referred to as *lama* (which became a term for a specific kind of Tibetan priest) or *vajra*, which means ... master. In my opinion, we can find things to learn about this practice from all these varied definitions.

Bhakti was an easier word, and it fit nicely ... because it was the word for the other side of the relationship equation. It is traditionally translated as "devotion", but the more modern American push is to translate it as "participation", meaning a fully engaged and deeply personal involvement with one's spiritual path. It is a form of worship whereby one conceives of the divine power in a human relationship with one's self, as a parent, friend, lover, or master to serve. *Bhakti* yoga, specifically, is a discipline of engaging with God/s in this deeply personal way. The word comes from the Sanskrit root *bhaj*, meaning "to share in", "to belong to", and "to worship". Some Western writers argue that "devotion" is a poor choice of definition for Westerners because the thought of "religious devotion" has become sterile and distant, and it does not give the proper connotation of the sense of deeply personal participation in the act of worship, or the ecstatic sense of love involved. I would argue that many modern consensual slaves would not have this difficulty.

I believe that words have power, and the most powerful words travel down an archetypal path; their multiple past and present meanings—even the ones only vaguely associated with them—collect around them, and much can be learned from them. Let's look at the major meanings I've listed from the etymology of this word. *From darkness into light. To praise. To raise up. To make a great effort. To share in. To belong to. To worship.* As I read these, they echoed in me, resonating with what we do in our path of spiritual M/s.

The urge to have power over another person can come from a very dark place. The urge to give oneself wholly can also come from a very dark place. Certainly the culture that we live in views it with suspicion, in the wake of many, many bad examples. To say that it is not dangerously prone to becoming unhealthy, on either side, would be a lie. To make it not only healthy but a vehicle for the greatest good and the furthest growth is a profound act of bringing light into the darkness. What spiritual SM does for the darkest urges of sex, spiritual M/s does for the darkest urges of relationship, dispersing the cultural darkness that has collected around it in favor of clear, open, ethical practice.

Part II: To Praise

Joshua:

I want be really clear that what we are talking about is a relationship with a master who is a human being. While doing *gurubhakti* only makes sense with a master that you respect and see as your spiritual superior in some way, they aren't God. Or rather, they are not the entirety of God. I happen to believe that all beings are manifestations of God, and that God is present in all beings. For me to worship God as manifest in this one person isn't to say this person is omnipotent, or omniscient, or infallible, or anything like that. I suppose it depends on your theology, but regardless, I think it is important to recognize that there is God beyond this one person, and this person might be really great, but they are not infallible.

(Even though I am a polytheist, I am intentionally using the term "God" in the capitalized singular because it has the most relevance and the strongest emotional impact on most people. If I say "your concept of divinity" or "higher power" or "the all-that-is" or even "Goddess", most Western people are able to approach it a lot more casually, as something "less-than-real-God", and that misses the point.)

It is important to fully understand your master's humanness and fallibility before doing starting a devotional practice. If you've only been together a few months and you think this person is perfect, it is almost impossible not to link the spiritual devotion to that illusion of perfection. In an impersonal relationship, as with most modern gurus, most people can maintain that illusion, but in an intimate relationship that is not possible. (Well, unless they are a saint or an avatar or something, and you know, I think even *they* have cranky days.) So if you still have that illusion of perfection, when something happens that forces you to confront your master's humanness, the intensity of that devotion can add even more fuel to your feelings of betrayal and resentment. Coming to *bhakti* devotion with a full appreciation of this person's humanness yields a much more mature and resilient spiritual connection, one that can withstand the ups and downs of life.

During the active practice of *bhakti* devotion, however, you don't focus on that humanness. You accept it is there, but it is irrelevant. You focus on the person's "Higher Self", the part of them that reflects divinity. You don't sit there and go through a list of all the great things about them, or what you love about them, or why they are worthy of your adoration. In that moment, you aren't evaluating them. You are just with them, experiencing them.

Raven:

Here I need to talk about the act of being an example. If the master wants the slave to struggle against great odds to perfect their path, to overcome their faults, to put their personal foibles and pettinesses aside for the sake of the goal, then they had better be modeling those behaviors themselves in their own life. It does not have to be toward the M/s relationship directly, although it can be. But we have found that watching the master strive selflessly toward a goal, while perfecting themselves along the way, is an amazing inspiration for the slave who is expected to do the same thing. It's not about whether it's fair, or tit for tat. It's about what works.

You can be worthy of being a master with no spiritual obligations whatsoever, so long as your slave thinks that you're an all right guy. When you add spirituality to the recipe, you are held to a higher standard. The Universe watches, and takes notes. When you add in the more complex level of *gurubhakti*, you need to understand that part of the guru job is being an example, a model—all the time. You can strive, you can even fail, but you must never give up. Remember the line from Bertold Brecht's spiritually cleansing poem *The Doubter*: "How does one act if one believes what you say? Above all, how does one act?" Being worthy of praise is acting that way. That includes: How does one act when one is stressed, or unhappy, or angry, or has erred, according to this worldview that I am teaching and modeling for my slave? Those are the most important times to model the right way to live in the world.

Part III: To Raise Up

Joshua:

The hardest thing for most people to get over with this sort of practice is that it needs to be taken seriously. It isn't that it is a grim or somber or formal kind of thing—it can be spontaneous and joyful. But the slave has to really mean it, in a deep and sincere way, not in a detached "I'm too cool for this" or "I'm too rational for this" kind of way. More than anything, that is the surrendering of the ego that most folks I've talked to need to be able to do this practice. If you've usually got a very irreverent attitude to your M-type (or to life in general), you need to be able to set that aside. Being reverent is what this is all about. You can use these practices to develop that reverence, but you need to be willing to go there.

First I want to be very clear that *gurubhakti* is not compatible with every spiritual tradition. Even within Hinduism, there are traditions where is it seen as appropriate to worship the guru as a manifestation of the divine, and there are traditions where that would be considered offensive. If you have sincerely-held spiritual beliefs or a strong investment in a particular religious tradition that would find worshiping the divinity within another human against their rules, this practice may not be for you.

Second, my understanding of the spiritual experience is strongly biased towards there being some type of a personal god that one can have a relationship with, a conversation with. I'm not saying that you can't do *gurubhakti* unless you share that understanding, only that it's challenging for me to explain it in a way that might make sense outside of that understanding. But I'll try!

I want to talk in fairly concrete terms about what "doing" *gurubhakti* looks like, but first I need to talk about the different places people might be approaching this practice from. There are two important questions here—whether there is a spiritual tradition that is personally meaningful to you, and whether you've had a deep emotional experience of spirituality within that tradition.

If you have a spiritual tradition that is personally meaningful to you, begin by using that framework. This is easier with some spiritual traditions than others, but I strongly encourage you to try. If your connection to that spiritual tradition is primarily social or cultural, it might be irrelevant to you, and that is okay. But if you have had any kind of spiritually meaningful connection to that tradition, I strongly encourage you to look for a way to integrate the two within your own mind and heart. (Whether you choose to share that understanding with anyone else in your spiritual tradition is entirely a different issue.)

If you don't have a strong connection to any spiritual tradition, you might still find value in exploring *bhakti* devotion as it is done in an existing spiritual context, in order to create your own. I think that it is easy to take a very superficial approach to a *bhakti* practice, and grounding it solidly in a coherently examined spiritual tradition is one way to stabilize a deeper connection.

Understanding *bhakti* devotion is easiest if you have already had a spiritual experience of this kind, where you felt the overwhelming presence of divine love. If you understand the heartfelt worship that naturally arises from that feeling of awe and adoration, then you know what state we are looking to evoke with this practice. If you haven't had this experience within some kind of spiritual or religious framework, it can be very difficult to find it for the first time with your partner. When people talk about "seeing God" in another person, they tend to assume we all know what "God" looks like. Well, maybe, maybe not. In an unmediated experience it is hard to mistake it for anything else, but it isn't so clear when your only experiences with it are all bound up with someone toward whom you have a wide range of strong feelings. Still, I can't imagine there is any actual harm done by practices that fall short of hitting that transcendent *bhakti* devotion, so there is no need to fear doing it "wrong".

Part IV: To Make A Great Effort

Raven:

I know that for many people, my talking about *gurubhakti* in a relationship which we label "master" and "slave" will sound like an incredible act of hubris. For others, it may sound downright cult-like. On the other hand, I am not looking to create waves of followers. I have only one follower, one person for whom I am explicitly the guru. One. And he signed up for it with open eyes.

Probably the first feeling that a reasonably self-aware dominant experiences when the slave attempts *gurubhakti* is a sense of vague inadequacy, or at the very least a thought of "Wow, this is a huge thing to live up to!" That's a normal and reasonable reaction, and it shows that they are actually thinking realistically about their position, instead of just treating it like an ego-aggrandizing game. It is an enormous expectation to live up to, and their job is to make that "great effort"—not to be perfect, but to never cease to strive toward that goal. As the slave kneels at your feet and consciously concentrates on seeing the divine connection within you, on seeing you as your higher self would have you be, something is put into motion in the Universe. You feel pressure, and not just from the slave, to be that higher self.

Gurubhakti isn't just about pressuring, though. It is about mutual manifestation. After a while, once you get over the initial reaction, you realize that your slave's conscious devotion to your higher self also begins to give you the wherewithal to make that great effort. If it's being done right, if you are both actually hitting that spiritual "groove", then the way begins to become clear for the master's striving. I experience it often as a penetrating serenity and clarity; while I still have the same life with the same number of problems, they don't seem overwhelming to me. *Gurubhakti* gives me an inner quiet, at least temporarily ... and, at times, both an urge to confront and improve my internal issues, and the inner resources to do so.

In most spiritual discussions of M/s, it's the master who is helping the slave along their spiritual path, guiding and improving them. The reverse is not done, because it is assumed that if the slave knew better than the master about how the master's path should be walked, they would be on an entirely different path together. The master is expected to make their "great effort" (or not, depending on how self-serving that particular couple's dynamic is) by themselves, with no help from the slave. I've always been down with that road, because I believe in spiritual masters taking responsibility for their own spiritual evolution, and no, I don't believe that my slave knows best. But I didn't know, before we began to practice *gurubhakti*, that the slave could actually have a practical effect on the master's evolution. To be clear, the slave does not concentrate on "making" the master connect with their own higher nature, nor attempt to push their intention on them. They simply kneel there and concentrate on seeing that divine nature, believing it as thoroughly as they can, and the Universe does the rest.

But you have to make the great effort. In one of the books that Joshua brought to me about *gurubhakti*, it listed a number of types of guru-disciple relationships, divided by the nature of the archetype that the guru manifested in the world. Some were parental—strict but loving, firm but fair disciplinarians who would call their followers on their illusions. Some were like children— innocent and wise, serenely engaging in their openness and honesty. Some were like playful friends, especially the "crazy-wisdom" gurus. Some were distant and mystical, like oracles or living votive objects. Some, the book said, manifested male and female energy in a balanced way and showed people how to do that in the world.

As a master, I resonated with the first archetype; as someone who works with transgender spirituality, I resonated with the last one. Either way, while his devotion uplifts me, I have to put my own will and commitment into the path. Only when I am fully doing that can I uplift him in turn. *Gurubhakti* is mutual great effort.

Part V: To Share In

Raven:

Joshua and I have spoken publicly about our concept of three kinds of service rendered by submissives or slaves: Transactional, Devotional, and Positional. Transactional service is done for a negotiated reward, Devotional service is done out of love, and Positional service is done because serving is an integral part of the server's identity. Transactional service is fairly self-explanatory, and we've written a good deal about Positional service because it's so closely a part of who Joshua is. However, we haven't said much about Devotional service, and we certainly haven't spoken about the far end of it. That's because it took us some years to fully understand what it looks like.

To serve and/or submit out of love can be a wonderful thing—or it can be something of a difficulty. There are ongoing arguments about the place of love in M/s—does it fall down as a motivation for the slave when they're angry at their master and don't feel love for them in the moment? Does it make the master prone to poor decisions—perhaps not being strict enough when it's needed? Does it get in the way? What about when the slave is in love and the master isn't? Some couples say that they can't imagine M/s without it, and look suspiciously at nonromantic M/s. Others mistrust it and their possible reactions were they to fall in love.

When people talk about love, they often bring up the "what do you mean by love, anyway?" question. We've found it useful to group Love by the three Greek definitions: *eros*, *philae*, and *agape*. *Eros* is romantic love: "being in love", complete with fireworks and all those brain chemicals that make you feel crazed desire and want to smell their hair all the time (because the brain chemicals are making you respond to their pheromones). *Philae* is "family" love: brother, sister, parent, tribe, best friend ever. People talk about their "leather family" or "leather tribe" sometimes in this demographic in the same way. Then there's *agape*, which is transpersonal love—seeing the "highest self" of the person you're looking at, and loving that, regardless of their actions in the moment. *Agape* is both more distant and impersonal and more compassionate and unconditional than either of the other two.

Think of these three forms of love as a triangle. It's easy to imagine the axis between *eros* and *philae*, between romantic and family love. It's also not so hard to imagine the axis that blends from *philae* to *agape*—one can envision the warm but somewhat selfless and self-sacrificing love that (ideally) occurs between parent and child. But the third axis is more difficult. How does one envision the middle ground between the deeply personal, romantic *eros* and the impersonal, spiritual *agape*? For us, this axis is where *bhakti* lives.

Joshua:

Some people, despite their sincere and meaningful connection to a particular spiritual tradition, haven't ever had a deeply emotional experience of that faith. Some spiritual traditions emphasize emotional experience more than others, and some people aren't naturally inclined towards this sort of experience. I really do believe you can more easily come to a genuine expression of *bhakti* devotion with your partner if you've first experienced it in a more obviously "spiritual" way, but some people may need to come at it from the other direction, starting with the personal love and opening to the transcendent aspect of that. How you get there doesn't really matter, but if you are having trouble getting there, and this makes any sense at all in your personal understanding of spirituality, ask yourself, "What would it feel like to fall madly in love with God?" Forget that there is any distinction between personal and transcendent love, and just try it. That is what *bhakti* devotion is, at its essence. I can't possibly explain what steps to take to fall in love with God, but my impression is that 90% of the process is just being willing and opening your heart.

Part VI: To Belong To

Raven:

This meaning struck me particularly when I came across it. What is more indicative of a master/slave relationship than to say, "You belong to me," or "I belong to you," and actually mean it in a way that is more than metaphorical? The feeling of being held and possessed can be a gateway to setting aside the ego. In the other direction, it can be a gateway to being moved to care for, to tend, to guide the soul who offers such raw vulnerability.

Joshua:

A person who devotes their life to a guru is called a *chela* or *shishya*. The terms are sometimes used interchangeably, and both are commonly translated as "disciple". The term *shishya* is the one used in connection with describing the lineage, the chain from teacher to student stretching back through time, each guru being the *shishya* of his own guru and so on. The term *chela*, however, comes from the Sanskrit term for "servant" or "slave". Of the two terms, it is the one that most emphasizes the concept of completely surrendering to one's guru, of obeying without hesitance, of turning over your will in its entirety. Often there is an emphasis on the spiritual value of surrendering the ego, and that process is exceedingly difficult to do without some kind of external guidance. The ego, being clever and intent on self-preservation, creates all manner of compelling justifications and explanations and exceptions to keep you from really facing your shit and doing the hard work that needs to be done. A guru is someone who can call you on this type of thing, but only if you are willing to listen.

In the traditional understanding of the *guru-chela* relationship, it is assumed that while a guru may be strict with his students, he never takes unfair advantage of them, and any hardships he inflicts on them are for their own good. Traditionally these gurus were often *sadhus*, renunciates who owned little besides a bowl and a single garment, and perhaps some ritual items. They clearly were not amassing wealth and power at the expense of their handful of disciples. But both in India and in the West, we now hear of "gurus" who do abuse this relationship, and this has caused many sincere gurus to question the appropriateness of the full expression of the *guru-chela* relationship in modern times.

Raven:

Master/slave relationships are also heavily scrutinized and mistrusted in our current culture, with similar worries about abuse. The guru and the master have similar pitfalls of arrogance and out-of-control behavior; the *chela* and the slave similar responsibilities for being discerning about who they give themselves to. We've often found, though, that when you claim a M/s relationship is spiritual, the Universe intensifies its scrutiny of you—and when you don't walk your talk, you fall much more quickly on your face.

Part VII: To Worship

Joshua:

To do any of these practices, it is important to be in the right frame of mind. In fact, the frame of mind is the whole point, and in a sense, once you've got the right frame of mind you don't actually have to do anything. However, it is good to do *something*. It helps bring one more solidly there, and once the pattern is established, the actions themselves can help bring about the right mindset. I'll use three examples from Hindu worship, but you can likely figure out similarly effective practices from any tradition.

Begin with both people doing some kind of preparation that makes sense to them, either together or separately. It can be saying a prayer, meditating, taking a shower and putting on nice clothes, whatever action says to you, "and now I'm going to do something spiritual". The attitude that the s-type is cultivating is reverent, loving, and joyful. It isn't a "groveling abject slave" frame of mind. It is closer to, "Being near you makes me so happy I can barely contain myself." or "I am overwhelmed with how wonderful you are." There are other attitudes appropriate to worship, but this is specifically a *bhakti* devotional practice. During the practice, the s-type strives to feel the radiant presence of God, and see their M-type as a manifestation of that presence. The M-type cultivates an attitude that is reverent yet assured, something like, "I am a worthy and fitting vessel of God. To honor me is to praise the glory of God." (For some people, this attitude comes naturally, for others it is more of a challenge.) The s-type can also do *bhakti* devotion to the M-type without the M-type doing anything at all. The first two practices I'll describe are reciprocal, the third isn't.

One of the key aspects of Hindu worship is "taking *darshan*". This is seeing and being seen, on a deep level, by the object of worship. It is a moment of intense spiritual connection, and is often the culmination of temple worship. With a guru, this is more than just making eye contact. It is seeing them, seeing deep into them, and seeing far through them, all at once, while they do the same. There is also a practice called *tratak*, gently gazing at something for a prolonged period. In the context of sexual Tantric practice, the practice is to sit with one person in the other's lap, facing each other, and gaze into each other's eyes. Other positions are fine, but this one is traditional. This isn't a staring contest—the gaze is soft—but you are actually looking into their eyes—or at least one of their eyes—not at their whole face or their forehead or nose. Being able to do this without feeling awkward is a very big step towards being able to unselfconsciously hold a reverent headspace toward your partner. *Darshan* is a more intense connection than *tratak*, and generally much briefer. *Tratak* is something you can just do any time. For it to be *darshan*, there needs to be not just a connection between the two people, but a palpable connection to God.

Some people can make that connection consistently, but for most people (at least at first) it is something that either arises spontaneously, or doesn't. If you can make that connection reasonably consistently, a very simple interaction involving *darshan* is this: the master sits, and the slave kneels at their feet, in prayer, with their head on the ground. When the master feels the time is right, they put their hand on the slave, who sits up. They make eye contact, for as long as seems appropriate, and then the slave returns to the floor.

Another key element of Hindu worship is *prasad*, the eating of blessed food, often sweets. Food is given to the object of worship, who blesses it and gives some or all of it back to the worshipper, infused with divine energy. This is a simple and very beautiful exchange, evoking the concept of taking one's nourishment from the object of worship, and taking the object of worship into oneself. One way of using this practice in M/s *gurubhakti* is for the slave to prepare some small special food and present it to the master, who holds the food for a moment and then feeds the slave. For some people, it may be more powerful to do this in a very formal way, with specific language. For some people it might feel awkward or unnatural, and they might prefer a less formalized interaction. You might start with something formal, and then scale it back to a very simple exchange, or you might start with something simple and gradually incorporate more formal elements as they begin to feel less awkward.

Another way of incorporating this element in M/s involves oral sex, but I think that way is actually very challenging to do correctly when you don't yet have a solid feeling of the basic interaction. It has always bothered me that in SM slang, "worship" can almost always be translated as "thoroughly licking". They aren't mutually exclusive, but they are by no means the same thing.

A third form of worship, and one that is very closely associated with *bhakti* practice, is devotional singing. Songs of joyful surrender and devotion are found in many religious traditions. One song from the Hindu tradition, *Mere Gurudev*, is specifically a devotional song to one's guru, and it begins, "My guru, I offer these flowers of my faith at your feet, whatever I have, you have given to me, and I dedicate it all to you." A few years ago at the Southwest Leather Conference, the main ritual included a song from the Christian tradition, "As the Deer", which begins, "As the deer panteth for the water, so my soul longeth after You. You alone are my heart's desire, and I long to worship You."

If you can find songs that speak to you in this way, it can help to create the right mindset to listen to them. (Feel free to change the words around a little if some lines don't work for you.) It is best to actually sing them out loud. Even singing them quietly when you are alone, or singing along with the recording, has more of an effect on your brain than passively listening. Singing to your master is the fullest expression of this practice. Even if you are not musically inclined, you might experiment with this. If it seems too awkward, set it aside for a while, and come back to it at a later date.

Raven:

I sit there with him at my feet, and my eyes meet his. I can feel that he is seeing me at my highest potential—not just imagining what it might look like, not just thinking about how nice it would be if I was a better person, but honestly doing his best to see through my everyday, mortal, flawed self to the part of me that touches the Divine Force. At some point, eye to eye, it came home to me—this is how the Universe sees me. This is how the Gods see me. This is what they see.

And I am struck with awe, and then a deep and abiding gratitude, and then an even deeper peace, the serenity and clarity that I spoke of earlier. And then after that, a great love wells up in me for him. It is not exactly the same fierce, possessive love that I normally experience for my slave, although it is not entirely alien to that sensation. It is like clear, warm water rather than a tumultuous stream. It comes through me, from beyond me ... from that place that my slave, my *chela*, sees that is through and beyond me. He reaches up and I take his hands, and it passes back from me to him.

I teach, and I am Seen. He learns, and he is Seen.

The Universe teaches both of us, in turn.

The Yin-Yang and the Tree: Two Models For a Spiritual Power Dynamic

Raven Kaldera and Joshua Tenpenny

When we first began speaking in public about our commitment toward M/s as part of our spiritual path, and began to work out what that looked like and how to communicate it to others, our experiences were intensely personal. How this worked for us colored many of our assumptions about how it worked in general, if only because there were so few accessible models. However, as we met and talked with other couples (and triples) who were finding their own ways along the path, we noticed that the structures holding the spiritual energy in its place in the M/s relationships often differed from ours. There were many things in common, but some overarching patterns were very different indeed.

After a while, we began to notice that the various spiritual M/s relationships tended to fall into two basic patterns. Raven chose to call them "the yin-yang" and "the tree" as metaphors for how the energy moved in each relationship. (If the word "energy" is too woo-woo for you here, replace it with "effort" or "time and attention".) Neither is good, bad, or better than the other. Each M/s couple will gravitate into what is most comfortable for them. It's possible to do either of them wrong, but it's also possible that if you're strongly ensconced in one, looking in on the other from the outside can cause you to imagine "They're doing it wrong!" when in actuality, they are merely doing a different path right.

The Yin-Yang

In the Yin-Yang model, the slave gives energy to the master, who transforms it and gives it back to the slave. The focus of the relationship, the hub that it rotates around, is mutual transformation and development of themselves as master and slave, and as people. Often the M/s relationship is the most important thing in their lives, the central point of their existences. One imagines the eternal interlocked circling of the Yin-Yang symbol—each providing something crucial and transformative for the other. The master directs the energy, but it is still very much a mutual effort.

The Yin-Yang is easier for a M/s couple to start out with than the Tree, because it encourages bonding and focuses both parties on perfecting the relationship. It's especially easier for most slaves, because it gives them lots of attention. The energy is contained within the relationship and does not leak out, so both parties are less likely to get burned out. On the other hand, it can become a reason to isolate, and/or to neglect other areas of life. Whether this kind of intense isolated focus is the correct spiritual path for both people is something that should be carefully evaluated, and reevaluated on a regular basis. (Sometimes the easiest path isn't always the one that the Universe wants you to take.)

The Tree

Imagine a tree. The roots take up energy—sustenance—from the Earth, and pass them up through the trunk to the branches and leaves. Then fruit grows, and falls to the earth, or is plucked by humans and animals. An immense amount of energy goes into that fruit, which will go away into the world and benefit others, and the tree will never see that energy again. That's the model for this structure. Generally, in a Tree relationship, the master has some kind of Great Work that is his calling, and which dominates his whole life. The slave's job is to support him in whatever way is necessary while he does that Great Work, basically serving the Work as well through him. The slave is the roots that feed the master's branches and leaves, and the fruit is the Work that goes out as a gift to the world.

Being in a Tree relationship is much more difficult for most slaves than a Yin-Yang structure. Everything is sublimated to the Work, and it may come before the relationship itself in importance. The slave gets much less attention, and the emphasis for both master and slave is on becoming better tools, not bonding or perfecting each other or their mutual path. We generally recommend that M/s couples start out with Yin-Yang relationships in the early stages, when they're still working out not only their dynamic but their mutual spirituality. However, occasionally a slave signs up with a master who is already ensconced in their Great Work, and they are stuck with a difficult learning curve.

On the other hand, occasionally one finds a slave who does better with a Tree structure than with a Yin-Yang. These are usually strongly service-oriented people who are more fulfilled by useful work than by attention and control (although they may enjoy that as well). We remember the words of such a slave who had a brief and unsatisfactory relationship with a Yin-Yang master: "I'm not broken, I don't need your healing, just give me something useful to do!"

Not Just A Duality

When both master and slave (or dominant and submissive, or whatever label or level of dynamic intensity they may have) prefer the same structure, everything can be worked out. The problem is when they are not well matched in this. The counterpart to the slave in the last paragraph is the one who would blossom in a Yin-Yang relationship, but the Tree structure makes them feel abandoned and devalued: "I didn't give my life away to be ignored and used as a workhorse!"

Of course, not every couple is one or the other one hundred per cent the time. Some couples shift between the two in different parts of their lives. Even a committed Tree couple with an all-encompassing Great Work need to periodically take some Yin-Yang time for the sake of relationship maintenance. On the other side, a Yin-Yang couple might throw themselves into a short-term project and utilize the Tree structure for a short time. Yin-Yang couples might also find themselves in the common situation where outside circumstances—work, illness, etc.—conspire to prevent them from concentrating on their relationship to the extent that they would like. Rather than backing off from their

M/s dynamic, they might find it more useful to restructure things as a Tree for the time being—"You and I are a team, and we're going to work together to get through this."

The Balance Of Sacred Archetypes
Aniel and Luluwa

In our relationship, Aniel is dominant and Luluwa is submissive. Our current power dynamic of the relationship is based on the archetype of a Prince (Aniel) and bound concubine (Luluwa). Essentially, the Prince is Owner and the bound concubine is property. Each part of the dynamic, for us, represents a spiritual element. The Prince is the controlling and organizing power; the concubine is the environment and the element in that environment which desires to be controlled. In the archetypal system of our spiritual practice, the "masculine" represents the center of self that looks out upon the "feminine" universe, and which reaches out and desires to control that universe. The "feminine" world at first resists, and the "masculine" takes action to conquer. In this dance of dominance and submission, each element finds its role. When the "masculine" conquers that universe, he becomes the Prince. The universe is bound to his Will, which becomes his realm, concubine and mate.

This is the spiritual basis of our dynamic, but it references powers that are the backdrop to this stage—Samael and Lilith, God and Goddess archetypes that have deep meaning to us. These are so important to us that we each have taken them on and integrated them into our consciousness. To varying degrees, depending on scene and ritual space, we manifest these spiritual archetypes and consider ourselves to be personifications of Samael and Lilith.

There are various stories and myths that describe the nuances of their relationship. The ones we have chosen, the ones that are most meaningful to us, represent the power dynamic described above. The power dynamic works as described based on the myths; however, Samael conquers Lilith because she willingly submits at a point in this deep fundamental story. Each partner in this story chooses their role as a manifestation of their True Will and essential nature. When we are in deep ritual space, we are Samael and Lilith. In more "mundane" or less highly charged scenes, and in day-to-day interaction, we are Aniel and Luluwa. Aniel and Luluwa are representative powers or energies of Samael and Lilith. However, the energies of Aniel and Luluwa, though not negated, are scaled to appropriately work with the day-to-day world. They are the face that Samael and Lilith show to the world.

We see our relationship as Prince and bound concubine in this spiritual context. Anyone from alternative lifestyle communities looking at us from the outside, especially the BDSM community, would see us as a 24/7 Master/slave dynamic that they think they would recognize. They would not see the spiritual dynamic that our relationship is based on unless they become involved in our "world".

Aniel:

I am a Thelemite and a practicing Zen Buddhist. I have been studying Thelema since 1989. (Thelema is a religious philosophy founded by Aleister Crowley in the early 20th century.) I entered what was to be a string of Thelemic orders in 1993. Though I have been reading on Buddhism since my teens, I didn't start *zazen* until 2005. I am also influenced by the belief systems that I have tried and passed through. At 13, I discovered Wicca and Neo-Paganism, and I still did Pagan "things" even after I started studying Thelema, but my participation in the Pagan community faded. Wicca and Neo-Paganism still have a place in my heart because they were my start in Magick, though I no longer hold to their tenets and beliefs. Other major influences are Taoism through the practice of Tai Ch'i Chuan and Ch'i Gung, and a myriad of elements from Hermeticism, the Western Mystery Tradition, Gnosticism, and Sufism.

As a Thelemite, I have a relationship with the deities **Nuit, Hadit,** and **Ra Hoor Kuit,** taken on as part of my initiatory and magical development as a Thelemite. On Samhain 1995 I ritually took on as my personal deities

Lilith the Bride of Demons, Samael the Archangel of Death, and Lucifer the Son of Morning. Each of these is a source of power and wisdom for me, my guides and a source of my Magick. At this point, I am 44 years old. Considering I started this process at 13, that means I have been on this path for 31 years. It is an ongoing process.

Luluwa:

I hold my personal beliefs to be very eclectic. I was originally raised in a Judeo-Christian belief system with bits of metaphysical philosophy thrown in for good measure, and I experimented with many beliefs over the years. Orthodox Judaism was my birth religion; from there I tried Satanism, Christianity, and Wicca. In addition to these, I researched many other paths including Islam, Buddhism, the Unitarians, Asatru, Druidry, Native American religion, and many others. I have slowly picked up bits of each religion on my winding path, along with various philosophies and scientific principles, and integrated them into a very personal belief system. Very strong influences on my beliefs have come from Paganism, Kahlil Gibran's *The Prophet*, *The Celestine Prophecies*, Observer-Created Reality from quantum physics theory, Neuro-Linguistic Programming, and *The Law of Attraction*. I have been told that my religious views are very Buddhist in nature. I can find comfort and truth in any belief system, making my spiritual practices very adaptable. I see every belief as inherently connected to one another—for me, the sacred is everywhere and accessible to everyone if they would only look for it.

From my involvement in the Neo-Pagan community, I find ritual very useful in connecting individuals on a spiritual level to accomplish a single goal. For instance, the invocation of Deity in ritual during a scene, especially when the nature of the Deities are drawn into the participants, is a particularly powerful way to integrate a form of role play in a power exchange. In 2005, I invoked the archetype of Lilith into me in a very powerful ritual and on a very personal level. This has had a very beneficial effect on my life, but it has caused many changes as well. Lilith has guided me to be a strong and self-confident person. While this may not seem to be in line with being a slave, it has helped me to be strong in submission, increased my self-esteem, and allowed me to become the person I was always meant to be. I am confident and secure in knowing that I desire to be of service, and in so knowing, I feel that her influence on my life has made me a better submissive.

Our D/s dynamic is central and core to our spiritual paths. As we interpret the relationship of Samael and Lilith that also aspects through Aniel and Luluwa, it is played out in our daily lives. So in essence, the D/s relationship is our Path.

We originally met one another when Luluwa was 16 and Aniel was 24. At the time, there was no intimate relationship, but the connection was made. Aniel made a conscious choice not to pursue an intimate relationship because Luluwa had not yet reached the age of consent, but a friendship evolved over the next few years, culminating in an intimate relationship when Luluwa was 21. During this time Aniel and Luluwa had a couple of mutual friends—a Master and his collared slave—who would later profoundly influence our views of a working and loving M/s dynamic. The relationship between us evolved over the next year, but then many events unfolded and put insurmountable barriers between us. These included responsibilities to Aniel's birth family, and for Luluwa a move and a relationship status change from polyamory to monogamy. We never had an opportunity to end the relationship, or even to say goodbye. The universe made certain of this—Aniel lost all contact information and Luluwa lost her telephone book as well.

It was during this 14-year separation that we came to know our True Will and grow into perfect companions for one another. We each travelled parallel paths, even going so far as having friends in common during this 14-year period, all without reconnecting to one another.

At 16 (and even at 21), Luluwa was still learning about herself and newly on her spiritual path. She was quite dominant in her day-to-day life. However, she is and has always been very service-oriented. Through a mostly-monogamous thirteen-year relationship, she learned how to sublimate her own desires for those of her partner. After the end of that relationship, she was formally introduced to the D/s lifestyle and trained as a submissive, and eventually evolved into a collared slave to a very competent and compassionate Master. While the universe orchestrated an end to their M/s dynamic, they continue to remain good friends.

At 24 (and 29), Aniel was quiet, reclusive and unsure of himself, and had difficulty navigating personal relationships. Growing up, from pre-adolescence onwards, he had consistent desires and dreams that involved BDSM. He eventually grew into his role as a Dominant through the evolution of several relationships, each of which gradually increased in intensity, power, and complexity. In the relationship prior to his reconnection with Luluwa, the female submissive was intended to be a collared slave, but instead taught Aniel what he definitely did *not* want in a slave.

The universe, in its infinite wisdom, then sought to reunite us to continue on our life's path together. Going through old photographs, Luluwa found a set from fourteen years prior where Aniel had been drawing on her back, and this inspired her to make an inquiry of the universe as to the whereabouts of Aniel. The inquiry manifested as an Internet search through which they found one another again. Unbeknownst to her at the time, Aniel had done a ritual to Lilith asking for his perfect mate only a month before. Upon further discussion, it was found that there were no less than six ways that we would have reconnected within the coming months—Aniel had been searching for three social groups with the exact same topics as the ones Luluwa was running; Luluwa had picked up a business card for the Thelemic Order that Aniel is in; and we had even attended the same Pagan Pride Day events five years in a row without really seeing one another. (One of those years, Aniel did see Luluwa at Pagan Pride day, looked away for a moment, and she was no longer there when he looked back up.) From that point, we had to wait several more years before the universe decided it was actually time for us to fully reconnect. Two weeks after that happened, Aniel found Luluwa's contact info as it fell from somewhere in his closet, and Luluwa found the long-lost telephone book.

Upon further reflection, many other synchronicities have come to light. Luluwa had stated to the universe that she would not enter into another D/s relationship with a stranger, and the universe responded by providing the one person from her past that she trusted with her life. Astrologically, we both have many similar and complementary aspects in our charts, including a stellium in the same Sun sign with our Suns conjunct as well as the planet Venus conjunct between our charts. Our bodies are also synergistically connected to the point that we suffer the same afflictions and heal at the same time as one another. Also, we find that we are intimately aware of each other's thoughts—one will think of an idea and a moment later the other will mention it, essentially completing each other's thoughts. The synchronicities extend even into our childhood experiences and patterns.

Given this connection and past, our D/s relationship has evolved easily and fluidly, with each learning the other's nature. Besides learning physical and psychological aspects, whether through play or the D/s practices of daily life, our spiritual natures have begun to evolve into a united path. We are each taking aspects of our own personal spirituality and applying it to the relationship. Aniel has primarily brought concepts from his Thelemic orientation, with the emphasis on each of us following our own True Will. Luluwa has brought the eclecticism of her magickal past to give the relationship shape and form. For us, every aspect of our lives is a manifestation of the spiritual and sacred because of our intertwined natures, our True Wills, and our own personal choice to be in this D/s dynamic.

With the powers of Samael and Lilith intimately connected with our consciousness, we tend to play our roles out for the most part without consciously thinking about it. In Aniel's daily magickal practices, whether Resh, *zazen* or conscious personal meditations on his Deities, he reinforces the powers of his nature—especially the Magician who seeks to dominate his world through becoming one with it, a union with the All. He also gives Luluwa instruction for daily practice such as meditation and ritual.

According to *The Book of the Law*, "Every man and woman is a star." Therefore, to each individual essence, all being is equal. However, every individual has their own unique path or True Will which gives them their unique expression. An individual's expression, for example, can be either dominant or submissive. So, in expression, the Prince is the spiritual superior because that is his True Will. The concubine is the spiritual subordinate because that is her True Will. We each have pursued our own spiritual path and have ended up at approximately the same place—while we have our own separate beliefs, they are synergistic in nature. When using our beliefs in scene or during ritual, we incorporate and interweave elements meaningful to both of us— but in the end, it is the Prince's decision as he is sovereign.

Aniel:

I have found that in order to succeed in being a dominant in a spiritual dynamic, I have had to deal with this obstacle: when circumstances want to break you, it is time to remember to trust yourself. I believe that there needs to be a fundamental confidence of the self to achieve spiritual mastery. When I say the "self", I mean your ultimate essence, which at its core is *Hadit*. You must trust your spiritual nature. The goal for a Thelemite is first knowledge and conversation with the Holy Guardian Angel which is your own personal connection with the spiritual essence of the Universe ... and eventually, the ultimate goal is oneness with the All. With this emphasis, the dominant is not just thinking of the mundane elements of the D/s relationship, but its use as a path to enlightenment.

Luluwa:

I believe that the most important qualities in spiritual service are to always be aware of the spiritual nature of the relationship, and to always be ready to serve. There are constant reminders of the bond we share, whether it be as mundane as both of us having the same aches and pains, or as esoteric as knowing the other is in a difficult place emotionally without them even being in the room.

Spiritual service is not only meant to be shown to my Prince. Spiritual service, for me, also means being of service to the universe, all the time. Sometimes this manifests as simply being at the right place at the right time. Other times it may manifest as a call for help in the middle of the night. Before I ever accepted myself as a submissive, I agreed to be of service to the universe. Actually, my service was demanded of me, and I fought it tooth and nail at first, and reaped the consequences. Accepting this was the hardest obstacle for me. When I finally came to a place of accepting it as my True Will, life began to flow easily. Just as I reaped the consequences as I fought my true destiny, I have since reaped the benefits and pleasures of being of service to the universe with joy in my heart.

Spiritual service to my Prince is no different. Every act is a spiritual event. While many may see service as mundane, for me it is not. Love is a spiritual state, and when you are of service to another with love in your heart, every action you do is an act of love, and every act of love is a representation of devotion to the one you serve. There is no greater joy than to be of service in every sense of the word.

The obstacle that is second hardest to being of service to the universe would have to be reconciling the integration of Lilith with being a bound concubine/slave in day to day life. There are times when the energy of Lilith within me is so strong that it does not want to submit. Finding the balance point within my being to allow both parts to coexist can be quite challenging.

For us, a non-spiritual power dynamic focuses on the people involved in the dynamic and their needs and wants on a purely physical, emotional, and intellectual level. The spiritual dynamic takes the individuals involved and gives them reference to, and unites them with, something greater than themselves. This "something" puts the D/s relationship in the context of what is happening in the rest of the universe. In that universe, there is a fundamental interaction of power that is represented by various aspects of dominance and submission. The interplay of dominance and submission in the universe is mirrored in the spiritual power dynamic.

It is important that anyone seeking a spiritual power dynamic must share the goals of the potential partner. You need to examine whether you really have the particular spiritual nature— either dominant or submissive—necessary to commit to these goals. Your expectations of what it is to fulfill these roles must be compatible with each other. This entire process demands trust, love, and commitment, and the willingness to choose this path.

Secondarily, it is important that your belief structures do not conflict on important points. If there are differences, you both need to be flexible. Obviously, the submissive is expected to be flexible to the degree to which it has been negotiated for their role in the relationship—but beyond this, even though they are given control of the relationship, the dominant must expect that a certain degree of flexibility is needed, since circumstances are always changing. Because of the constantly evolving nature of a spiritual power dynamic, both partners need to have a willingness to learn from one another. It is important to not lose sight of the fact that a spiritual power dynamic is a partnership.

The most important thing to remember is that pursuing a spiritual power dynamic is not an easy path. The best way to deal with this is to obey your True Will. You do this by finding a spiritual practice that makes you observe and connect to your own spiritual essence. That connection is not a one-time thing; it is a path that is constantly evolving, and you need to constantly apply yourself to the process. The D/s relationship can be used to further the growth of both dominant and submissive. Finally, remember to continue to seek knowledge in all areas of your life, and never be afraid to try something new.

Arc and Covenant
Krittika and stardust

Krittika:

I sought for many years without knowing what I was looking for. Running on the beach and watching my shadow stretch before me in the starlight. Donning fighting gear and dancing with opponents in the ring. Hiking through bogs, the only path marked with white signposts that disappeared in the clouds that rolled off of the mountain. I did not know the name for spirituality, and the only road to God that I was taught did not take inner experience into account. Religion was a stern blonde woman with long red nails who snapped her fingers in our faces when we didn't pray loudly enough. Appearance and reality were words for the same shining garden. I spent many years walking its paths, building beautiful masks to wear at the dinner table.

On the surface, I was a shy, slim student with an intellectual bent. I got into the right college, played sports, and had everything that any nice young person should want. My hungers were an unexplored emptiness, and I'd safely locked my inner child in the basement, along with most of my monsters. One night when I was nineteen years old, an older man drugged me and tried to take my body away. How was he to know that though I looked female, my energy shifted between masculine and feminine, that in my fantasies I was as likely to be Top as bottom, Dominant as submissive? He tried to erase my sexual agency, and so I became determined to take it back. Golden tigers prowled behind my eyes, and men and women began looking over their shoulders when I passed them on the street.

By day, I studied psychology. At night the darkness called to me, and I answered. I began practicing BDSM, taking topping classes, and going to sex parties. Red tendrils of Domme energy flashed through the cracks of armor that covered my heart. I used my martial arts and theater background to learn how to "two-foot", using part of my awareness to monitor my partners' safety, and giving the rest up to erotic performance. A friend gifted me a black Remington hunting knife, and I learned how to run it over soft, vulnerable skin. Men knelt sobbing at my feet, and my monsters shivered with unholy joy. My body glowed with power as I danced at all-night raves. Reality was a garden where one could plot living artwork, and I was determined to grow roses the size of fists. It was at this point in my journey that I met the person who I would come to call stardust.

stardust:

My name is stardust. It is literally what I am. It reminds me of the span from the vast and glorious to the tiny and mundane. It also describes work I feel called to in this life, which is to bring starlight— silent, beautiful, profound—down to the earth.

My explorations of power exchange are necessarily spiritual, because I have lost the distinction between the sacred and mundane in my life. There was a time when I believed especially the meditation cushion, the softly polished wood of the temple, to be a more sacred place than the mainstream of modern-day America. Now, having journeyed into history and land in my tribal faith of Judaism, and the roiling currents of my own body and psyche through group energetic work, that simplistic line between spirit and the rest of life has been thoroughly twisted, tangled, and smudged. When I first encountered my Domme, the darker side of my sexuality was one of the last realms of my life that still lay outside this mandala. Now it, too, has been claimed.

The seductive pull of dominance and submission has always been present in my spiritual life as well. I have been drawn to the paths of devotion, pain, fearlessness. One of my most blissful months was in the icy winter of upstate New York. Early mornings were gliding in dark robes, aching knees from the stillness of long meditation. Relief came in digging sleet from the driveways, in dim gray light and wet yellow coveralls—or occasionally, from the sting of the kyosaku stick on the shoulders, as the monitor padded softly by. Yet the motivation was love, and the result was beauty. I cried silent tears in the zendo, from determination and the burning of my knees, and also from the gentleness, trust, and clarity of the community, and the simplicity of utter devotion to schedule, to training, to the teaching, to awakening.

In the dusty one-room synagogues of Jerusalem, I wound black leather straps around my arm, a sharp point of one tefillin box pricking my chest near the heart, and the other pressing down on my third eye, the solemnity of ancient words contained within them. Shivers on my skin, I contemplated the Ein Sof, *the infinite Without End, as if standing directly before me, and prayed out loud for the strength to find my way, not to give up on the repair of this broken world.*

In the midst of Manhattan, cheerful and relentless facilitators taught me to allow rage, terror, delight into my body in ways I had at some point in my life stopped tolerating. They encouraged, tricked, and cajoled me into pushing my breath into tight knots of muscle, exposing long-hidden shameful thoughts, and emaciated dreams, shaking, sweating, and sobbing, until the shadows were brought into full light.

Krittika:

When I first began playing with my boy, to say that it was not intended to be a spiritual pursuit would be something of an understatement. He was new to BDSM, and I enjoyed the thought of giving him a taste of bottoming and submission before he left for graduate school. I already owned a 24/7 slave, had a polyamorous boyfriend and girlfriend, and was not interested in anything more than a hot fling. However, my encounters with this boy felt qualitatively different than other play-dates. I topped him based on the parameters we negotiated; my tools included erotic pain and pleasure, psychological drama, physical ordeals, and role-playing with mythical archetypes. I understood that these could have deep psychological power, but believed that they only had the power that we chose to give them. I was an ethical atheist and scientist, and my worldview was based on a combination of empiricism and constructed narrative. Had I known what spiritual BDSM was, I doubt that I would have chosen to practice it.

I planned the story arc of our play partnership to encompass several scenes, each designed to open different paths into submission for him. The climax of the arc would be a public suspension, letting him spread his metaphorical kinky wings. Then we would amicably go our separate ways. With my slave boy and other submissive-types that I dated, our scenes were mostly focused on the erotic—to them, submission meant putting my sexual pleasure before their own. However, with stardust there was a depth to service that I had never felt before. His background in meditation made it easy to move him into altered mental states. He allowed me to wander through his mind and use his body in whatever way I saw fit—and something moved through me which knew how to care for him and guide him. Based on scientific research on the phenomenon of inspiration, this is probably a personal experience of evocation. In role, I did not think— something in me intuited. Out of role, I felt like a novice musician gifted with a rare, precious instrument, who knew just enough to feel the power and depth of the music that it could play.

stardust:

My arc with Krittika began where these years left off. One of the last stages of the energetics program was to enter into our sexuality. Having been acutely aware of my kinky interests since boyhood, I still alternately indulged them, held them at arm's length, or condemned them in myself. In the group, though, I allowed myself for the first time to be thoroughly physically and verbally dominated by the two members of my group to whom I felt the most raw attraction. The magnitude of the bliss I felt and the energetic release left me stunned, and sure that this was the next gate for me to enter.

It was as if by providence that I met Krittika just days later. The setting was a most innocent birthday party. Neither of us had a hint of what was to come, and yet something drew us to meet again. When we first discovered each other's predilections, we wrestled and tested each other. We relate as equals outside of our roles. There are times when I will top her, for sensation, body and soul care. Yet there is no question that this journey is for me, about entering into the realm of submission.

Krittika:

Though I've learned Risk Aware Consensual steps for playing with actual fire, there is always a risk of someone getting burned. No less so with other tools for BDSM—just because one doesn't believe in the Gods does not mean that these archetypes don't have a hold on the human psyche. I didn't realize that the work I was doing was spiritual, that the tools that I was using to open stardust were the same ones that people had used for thousands of years to induce transformative experiences. Rhythmic pain, trials of endurance, physical ordeals, confession, breath-work, energy work in the form of guided imagery—these were all things that I did instinctively with stardust during our first arc without knowing what doors that I was opening. Opportunities for learning were right in front of my face—I had performed with Lee Harrington at a steampunk ball, and occasionally read his blog—but thought that his experiences with Bear were the quirks of a talented visionary artist, like Yeats's automatic writing or Blake's angels. Luckily, stardust has a long history of spiritual exploration, as well as emotional maturity, and was not harmed by my greenness.

My yet-unnamed spirituality began to bloom when playing with stardust, but quickly bled into other encounters. I hooked up with a friend and we came by breathing together and staring each others' eyes. The orgasm began in my mind, connecting me with him and feeling oneness, and moved shudderingly down my spine, through my heart, through my stomach, to finally explode in a fiery white burst when our still-clothed cunt and cock simultaneously came. Experience built on experience, and within three months, as I sat and meditated, I had a vision where I lost my fear of dying, experienced ego death, and was gifted with new responsibilities through a shamanic patron. Then stardust supported me through two days of black depression as I tried to reconcile mysticism with my perspective as a scientist. Without the love and support of my girlfriend and stardust, I would probably have dismissed the entire experience as a temporary descent into madness. Finally, I accepted that there are many paths leading to different kinds of awareness, and was able to move forward. Luckily, my girlfriend had studied spiritual BDSM practices as part of her academic interest in psychology; as soon as she saw stardust and I interact in role, she gave us the proper name for our work.

The name that my boy has given me is Krittika. It is the Indian name for the star cluster also known as the Pleiades. In Sanskrit, it means "the cutters". My main tools for spiritual work are knives—the elegant black Remington which has carved out ritual space in my life, the tiny blades of needles, astral claws and teeth, and, from stardust, an iron *Kartika* for cutting through the veil of ignorance.

stardust:

Krittika is my Domme. We have channeled these names for each other.

I care for her by serving her needs, offering myself as a resource to her, inspiring her. She cares for me by pushing me, guiding me into what I need. She is the first person to whom I have offered ongoing submission.

Krittika:

Practicing spiritual BDSM as a Dominant encompasses three main tasks for me. First, I am the willful partner who chooses what direction our exploration will go. I've planned arcs for our play so that we can explore the aspects of BDSM that are most beneficial to both of our development. It's a way of narrowing the infinite possibilities that we could explore, and also a way to keep us from getting stuck in a rut, doing only what is fun or convenient. The process of crafting our arcs is a creative endeavor. By guiding how our scenes relate to each other, there is a greater sense of purpose to what we are doing. Arcs also suggest the natural cycle of inception, building, and release, like waves gathering to break on a shore. I like the feeling that submission is something that stardust must decide to give over and over again.

Each time I accept it, it's a new gift. In our latest arc, he has asked to collaborate with me in this planning process, and I have agreed.

My second task as a Domme is to be an energetic Top. I plan where a scene will take place and set up the chain to keep others out. I create space for my boy to submit to me, and push him to do so with all of his mind, heart, and body. I hang him in the air with ropes, beat him, caress him, fuck him, whisper stories in his ears, pour hot wax over his skin. I stay calm in the face of pain, trauma, tears, anger, and turmoil. I break open his energetic barriers, the walls of tension that his body creates to hide emotion, and give him sweet release. Topping feeds my own desires to take care, to give pain, to force pleasure, to open, to witness, and to be in control. I also occasionally top from the bottom—when I want an ordeal, energetic release, or to experience sensation, then I use stardust's skills as a service top to meet my needs, and give his monsters space to play.

My third task as a spiritual Domme is to channel love. I find it valuable to create space where love is not conditional on actions, but actions still have real life consequences. I am not stardust's Domme because I am morally better than him, stronger than him, or more deserving of power in any way. I am no more or less Divine than he is, and no more or less in integrity at any given moment. However, as Domme I am the final arbiter of punishment—his, and my own. I am the gatekeeper of demons, deciding how and when our monsters will come out, and how and when they'll be returned. And I am the Loving Dominant who brings 100% of my effort, and expects nothing less in return.

stardust:

Submission for me means surrender—through to the core. What I aspire to offer her is simple. Absolute willingness, openness, and presence.

Willingness means I carry out the task, regardless of my feelings, my own desires, my preconceptions. My role is devotee—it is her will that I carry out. Kneeling in the desert dust, afraid to scream at the top of my lungs, I let it rip anyway. Unable to lift my body, shaking, I strain to do one more pushup for her. Dazed from body blows, I grope for words to offer her my inner experience.

Openness means that I don't withhold even a sliver of myself. There is no refuge. I am hers, clear through. If she asks me the contents of her mind, I tell her—even if it is a former lover, an irreverent joke—especially if it is a shameful secret. Sometimes she feels the resistance in my body, and pushes until I let go. She excruciatingly digs into my sorest trigger points, bites my bound flesh, until I give up struggling. She pushes her cock into my choking throat until it relaxes. She slaps my face until I finally give up bracing myself or turning away.

Presence means attention. At all times, I strive to remain aware, responsible. In the midst of a flogging, a fucking, a meditative trance. If I notice a mundane worry, an embarrassment, a fear, a fantasy that is taking me away from presence, I tell her so she can bring me back. If I notice her entering top-drop, I ask if I can bring her the red meat and fruit juice that she thrives on. If I'm near to crossing an emotional line, I flag it for her, so she can choose to push me across, or keep me together.

It also means feeling everything. No dissociating. No gritting, enduring, shutting off sensation. One lesson here—pleasure can be easily as difficult to experience as pain. I have screamed as she relentlessly works my prostate, and the blinding sensations shudder through torso and limbs—my breathing coming in spasms, legs shaking, my throat choking up. She delights in my sensitivity, and I delight in the rawness of life that she awakens within me.

Krittika:

It has been one year since stardust and I began seeing each other. We're on our third arc, with an end point set for Yom Kippur 2011. Our spiritual explorations have incorporated Judaism, Buddhism, and shamanism. Our tools include art, BDSM practices, psychology, and meditation. Our play has taken us from sharing fellowship on top of a 12-story Manhattan building, to stardust screaming on his knees in the desert, to a sex party where my boy serviced anyone who wrote their request on my silver dessert platter. We touch fire: burning sexual passion—candles flickering against a summer night—the searing heat of shame on his cheeks—the transformative blaze of revelation—the warmth of my approving smile. We touch earth: practicing grounding after scenes—discussing ancestral roots—digging into the muck of old trauma—reveling in raw, earthy desire. We touch water: flowing with the currents of life—the shock of cold water on skin— exploring rivers of fantasy—melting the ice around our hearts. And, lastly, we touch air: flying free of bodies through astral play—following breath to be present—leaving the ground through ropes of red hemp--connecting with words across vast distances.

stardust:

To what end do we undertake all of this?

We explore energy. Pain, restraint, sexual touch drive incredible currents through my body, teaching me vividly where I am open and flowing, where closed and frozen. My concentration deepened by devotion to service, she guides my awareness through my chakras. Vivid images, light, fears run through me. Much of my particular work is to bring my higher awareness, where I would prefer to remain drifting peacefully in exquisite, holographic visions, into the muddy, overgrown chaos of the everyday, where visibility is one step ahead, and every detail is a wrench in the works. So she fearsomely grips me and pulls me down from my refuge in the blue-indigo of crown and third eye, into the tangles of my solar plexus, the red volcanic depths in my root.

We create beauty. Our bodies in different cities, our minds entangle, in an alternate astral world, where our play is free from physical limits. We alter and blend our gender, take on animal forms. I have lost count of the times I've given my body to her—felt my neck snap in her jaws, her claws through my chest, been run through by blades and arrows. What I will only experience once as a human, I can practice as a devotion here. The charge we feel is forged into words, poems, rope and ritual art.

We build virtue. I learn to restrain my impulses, to hold boundaries against temptation. Once, my assigned task was to ask her to stop if at any time during our play she touched her lips to my cock—

a powerful and practical training for maintaining safer sex practices in the midstream of desire and excitement. I learn integrity, seeing in sharp relief when I wish I could cut a corner, or give only 90%. I deepen my meditative discipline, holding the images, emotions, mental frames I am given: when offering my Domme floggings or sex as a service top, I go within to counteract appearances, and maintain my role as a submissive.

We play with monsters. I tend to feel acutely the darkness in this world—the cruelty, greed, loneliness, hunger and disease, war and abuse. The demons of violence and non-consent, of self-hatred and malice. They have been branded into each generation of young, soft hearts by the guilty hands of the last, since ancient time. My heart, too, has been branded. Like the bent growth of a tree trunk, these marks cannot be undone—only set to new purposes. So, in chains, I conjure my demonic cohort for Krittika to wrestle and dance. They, I, curse at her, spit, mock, shamelessly show all the cruelty and bile that my "good" side wishes away. I trick and look for openings—bound, I catch her off guard, steal her flogger and hold it underneath me, flicking it out to taunt. When Krittika herself seeks an ordeal she uses these monsters, as when baring the layers of her psyche to their judgment on the reflective day of Yom Kippur. Together, we become intimate with the forces we would otherwise deny, even as they subtly distort our lives.

Finally, we enjoy the moment, revel fully in our dewdrop existence as human beings. Joy is a factor of awakening. I seem to derive endless bliss from being a slut for her, being a toy, being used and enjoyed. Sometimes in a silly way, writhing as she tickles me mercilessly. Sometimes in a hard way, being pimped out at a party. Sometimes in a juicy way, with copious orgasms all around. Sometimes tenderly, simply feeling her within me.

Krittika:

Ultimately, spiritual BDSM has provided me a path to access part of human experience that I thought did not exist—that of divine presence. Mysticism had leaked out in my life before, but without a name, a path, or a purpose, it burst forth in incoherent poetry and existential angst. Finding a path that channeled these impulses in meaningful ways has been a blessing. Feeling universal love, and bringing it into my interactions with others, has deepened connection without impeding personal freedom. Feeling the unquantifiable tininess of human existence, the tides and energetic whirlpools of my body, the connection to every other part of the world, has brought new joy to my work as a scientist by deepening my reverence for the cosmos.

stardust:

All this, for me, is practice for living—meaning, being fully alive. Humans are not in charge. This world is immeasurably vast, immeasurably stronger than us. Our lives, our whole history, are tiny, iridescent ripples on its surface. Its forces will cause joy and pain, success and failure, birth, and inevitably death. We do not ultimately choose how or when these things come. In the face of this existential helplessness, the small i can dig its heels in, kick and scream, try to close off and deaden against it all, stop the merry-go-round. Or it let go and allow everything to move like wind through the channels of the body-mind. It can be open, present, and willing, and in so doing, end its self-imposed separation, and accept its unity and true relationship with the Big I. Surrendering to the world—trusting it and allowing it to be Dominant, giving up a pointless struggle for authority, simply responding to and accepting what comes—frees a living being to actually experience life.

Krittika is fierce. In my visions I often see in her as a dark angel, a destroyer goddess, kin of Kali, with skull and blade in hand. And I trust completely in the love that comes with her wrath. She has upheld that trust with respect, attention, tenderness in a thousand ways. We have both committed to loving each other, no matter what—whether we play together, whether we hurt each other, whether or not we like everything about each other, whatever form our connection takes. She is not infallible. She is equally as human and as divine as I am. What matters is that we have both committed to hold goodwill for the other in our hearts. This sense that she cares for me as fiercely as she plays with me is the essential foundation of our play. Without it, I would need to hold a part of myself back. With it, I can open myself, offer myself to another human being, completely.

Krittika:

If I had never met stardust, at some point in my life the threads would have woven together in a different tapestry; perhaps through renewal Judaism or tantric exploration, perhaps through a birth or a baptism, or perhaps at the moment of my death, a pattern would have emerged. However, sitting in my leather armchair with the memory of stardust's soft mouth around my cock, I am immensely grateful for the gift of my boy.

Called Deeper: Divine Service Through Ownership
Lee Harrington and Aiden Fyre

By tears, cum, sweat and joy, let our Work be our offering.

By North, echoing the strength of stone and bone, boot prints, and fists buried deep, let our Work be our offering.

By East, whispering our communication and desire, strangled moans, and whipping cane strokes, let our Work be our offering.

By South, lighting fiery passion and loving hearts, ecstatic screams, and ashy cigars, let our Work be our offering.

By West, carrying deep resonances and waves of emotion, squirting orgasms, and the scent of piss, let our Work be our offering.

Together we enter this working.

The first owned and in service to Bear, the mighty Neolithic force, whose rending claws wipe away illusions and whose every footstep tramples down fear; Bear who holds us tight as we open doorways and clear obstacles, and see ourselves in our full capacity and strength.

The other a child of Lilith in service to her, Queen of the desert and Goddess of destruction; Lilith the shapeshifter between genders, who opens us up to the mirrors of our shadow, and shows us the courage to push beyond our comfort and discard what no longer serves us.

Our Work is life.

Our Work is love.

Our Work is building something together that is greater than either of us could do alone.

When we look at our lives, the stacks and boxes, the Google calendars packed full and the to-do lists that seem to go on forever—it seems impossible. How can those we serve, our

Mothers, our Matron/Patron beings who have claimed us, demand so much? How can we possibly do it all?

Lilith's eyes flash—"Did I not send you a teacher? A guide?"

Bear's eyes flash—"Look."

Pausing, we breathe in and hear Their message.

We see before us amazing beings:

Owner, *Guru*, Sacred Gift...

Property, *Presadi*, Sacred Gift...

...and we see each other for all that we are.

Looking at our collective Work, we realize that with an ally, this Work is in fact possible. It is possible because we are not alone. It is possible; when we combine our efforts, we combine our focus into one. We take one path together.

This path we take together is called Ownership. Is called Sacred.

Do not mistake being alone for loneliness.

Being alone does not mean being unable.

This is not a thing of co-dependence.

This is the work of conscious interdependence.

Together or independent, we are powerful and amazing. Our culture's perception that an individual has no value without a better half—it is a fallacy. Without the other, our service to the world would still hold value, and our Work would still be our Work.

But we are called deeper—to dive deeper. To dive into and through fear. Called to pass the way-stations of apathy, spurring each other on further and deeper still.

And when we think we have taken our last step ... the mirror. My Property lifts up the mirror of their eyes, and I am reminded of my own Godhood, my own potential, my own Work.

My Owner lifts up the mirror of their eyes, and I am reminded of my own Godhood, my own potential, my own Work.

Sometimes, a reminder is all it takes.

Sometimes, it is a firm hand, a formal demand.

Sometimes, it is a soft hand, a gentle nudge.

By being in an Ownership dynamic, we unlock the doors to each others' hidden potential. We embrace the challenge and whisper the secret names of love.

Let Property not be locked away from the world. Let its greatness and power be heralded. Let it be free of emotional bondage—because when Property shows their greatness, it serves both its Owner and the world in our combined great Work. Let this be an investment that blossoms and grows.

Let Ownership not be a burden. Let its greatness and power be heralded. Let it be free of emotional bondage—because when an Owner shows their greatness, it serves its Property and the world in our combined great Work. Let this be an investment that blossoms and grows.

Together, we are able to dive deeper. By proving our capacity, we are called deeper into this sacred Work. Our Work on this planet and beyond is a sacred thing—because we are.

By tears, cum, sweat and joy, let our Work be our offering.

Holy Fire

Raven Kaldera

RAVEN KALDERA

This song was written for the interfaith service at the 2011 Master/slave Conference, as a choral anthem for M/s spirituality. It can be sung acapella, or if you want guitar accompaniment, the repeating chords are:

G C FC G
G C FC G
G C FC G
G C FC G G
D D C C G G
(Last chorus:)
D D C C G FC G FC G FC G G

About The Editor

Raven Kaldera is a queer FTM transgendered intersexual shaman. He is the author of too many books to list here, including *Dark Moon Rising: Pagan BDSM and the Ordeal Path* and *Dear Raven and Joshua: Questions and Answers About Master/Slave Relationships.* He and his slaveboy Joshua have been teaching and presenting workshops regularly for many years to the BDSM, Neo-Pagan, Sex/Spirituality, transgender, and other communities. 'Tis an ill wind that blows no minds.

9 780982 879429